D0082556

Photographs and Photographers

of

York

The Early Years
1844-1879

William Henry Fox Talbot, 1800-77. A carte de visite portrait made by John Moffat of Edinburgh in May 1866. *Trustees of the Science Museum, London*

William Pumphrey, 1817-1905, grocer, schoolmaster, photographer and asylum superintendent.

John Ward Knowles, 1838-1931. He practised for a short time as a professional photographer before turning to glass painting. *Mrs. Milward Knowles*

Joseph Duncan, 1820-95 and his wife Mary Ann, the widow of Mr. Lord. The top book on the table is *A Manual of Photographic Chemistry* by Hardwich, first published in 1855. *P. W. Hanstock*

PHOTOGRAPHS & PHOTOGRAPHERS OF YORK

The Early Years 1844-1879

by

Hugh Murray
M.A., C.Eng., M.I.E.E., M.C.I.T.

Yorkshire Architectural and York Archaeological Society
in association with Sessions of York

By the same author:

The Horse Tramways of York 1880-1909	1980
Dr. Evelyn's York	1983
Servants of Business	1984
Heraldry and the Buildings of York	1985

First published in 1986

ISBN 0 9503519 4 6

© YAYAS 1986

Printed in 10/11 Plantin
by William Sessions Limited,
The Ebor Press, York, England

Contents

Acknowledgements

ON 6 MARCH 1983, after I had spoken at a meeting of the York Roundabout Group, the chairman, Sydney Heppell, remarked that he had attended many talks on York over the years and thought he had seen all the old photographs of York that existed but he had been amazed to find many new to him among my slides, especially of Victorian York. This comment was particularly opportune as I was trying at that time to find a theme for a sequel to *Dr. Evelyn's York* which could be illustrated by further pictures from his priceless collection of lantern slides made for the many lectures he gave in his campaign to preserve York from 'ruthless commercialism'. Syd's remark provided the inspiration I was looking for and I am grateful to him, not only for this but also the help and encouragement he has given me in his other capacity as Keeper of the Evelyn Collection.

Having then decided that the book should present York through the eyes of Victorian photographers a possible refinement occurred to me as I sought material in the Collection. This was to concentrate on the early years of photography and the photographers who mastered the techniques of the new science and demonstrated by their results that it could also be an art form. My searches for their work led me out of York to London, Edinburgh and Aberdeen – to the Science Museum, the Royal Scottish Museum, the Scottish National Portrait Gallery and the University of Aberdeen and I acknowledge the assistance given to me by the custodians of the photographic collections at these places.

The final result would have been immeasurably poorer without the contribution of Peter Hanstock. His parents both practised as commercial photographers at 11 Clarence Street and consequently he has an expertise in photographic practice in the days of glass plates – well before the advent of the SLR camera and 35mm film. Besides his advice on techniques and processes he has allowed me to select from his collection of glass negatives made by Joseph Duncan. Some of these have suffered the ravages of time but Peter has used his artistic skills to remove blemishes and paint in damaged details with such precision that they cannot now be detected.

In my efforts to date the pictures from internal evidence and to provide material for the captions I have been, as always, unstintingly helped by Maurice Smith and his staff at York City Reference Library and Rita Freedman and Mary Thallon in York City Archives.

The result is a book that tries to fulfil several purposes simultaneously; the early history of photography in York, the identification of the photographers and the photographs they took in the City in this period and, lastly, a photographic record of York in the 35 years after the taking of the first known picture of one of its buildings. The collection made by Dr. William Arthur Evelyn, albeit for an entirely different reason, has proved to be an invaluable starting point for all these objectives.

This starting point would certainly not have been reached without the motivation of Florence Wright. Sadly she died on 7 June 1986, only weeks before publication, having been a member of The Yorkshire Architectural and York Archaeological Society for over 53 years and a tower of strength in its activities for much of this time. This book is then, first and foremost, a small acknowledgement of her friendship, her work for the Society and her love of the City of York.

HUGH MURRAY   YORK 1986

1 Introduction

BY A STRANGE COINCIDENCE the two rival processes that marked the beginning of practical photography arrived in York in the same week. The calotype, the invention of William Henry Fox Talbot, was brought from Scotland by David Octavius Hill and Robert Adamson who came to take portraits of the eminent scientists who were attending the 14th annual meeting of the British Association for the Advancement of Science held in York between 26 September and 2 October 1844. An advertisement in the *Yorkshire Gazette* on 5 October announced that daguerreotype portraits were being taken daily at 50 Stonegate. These were the premises of Samuel Walker, an artist, who had just returned from London where he must have learnt the process and obtained a licence to practise it from Richard Beard, a coal merchant, who had opened the first commercial photographic studio in Britain in March 1841 at the Royal Polytechnic Institution. From there Beard, who was himself licensed by Louis Jacques Mandé Daguerre, sold to photographers in the provinces the exclusive rights to the process over a specified area – in York and for 20 miles around for Samuel Walker.

While the birth of photography as we know it today belongs to the nineteenth century, the light sensitive properties of certain chemicals which were to make it possible were known much earlier. In 1614 Angelo Sala had observed the blackening of silver nitrate when exposed to light and in 1727 a Bavarian, Johann Heinrich Schulze, captured the image of some letters on a suspension of chalk and silver in nitric acid contained in a glass bottle. In this country in 1800 Thomas Wedgwood of the pottery family made images of ferns, leaves and paintings on glass on paper coated with silver nitrate solution, but he was unable to devise any method of retaining or fixing his images. Daylight, by acting on the unused silver salts quickly turned the whole paper black. It was thus left to a Joseph Nicéphore Niépce, a French artist and amateur scientist, to produce the first permanent image. After first trying silver chloride without success he eventually discovered that bitumen of Judea hardened if exposed to light for a long period. He dissolved it in a suitable solvent and painted it on to pewter plate. This was covered with an engraving on translucent paper. Where light passed through the engraving the bitumen hardened but where it was shielded by the lines of the picture it remained soft and could be dissolved away by a mixture of lavender oil and white petroleum, leaving a permanent image on the plate. He used these plates in a *camera obscura* and, after an eight hour exposure to the light cast on its table, produced an identifiable image. His earliest surviving picture was made in 1827 and shows a very faint image of the buildings opposite his home at Saint-Loup-de-Varennes.

On 4 January 1829 Niépce made an agreement with Daguerre, who was also trying to record the images produced by the *camera obscura*, that they would work together to try to discover a more practical process. Niépce died in 1833 but his son, Isidore, continued to work with Daguerre. By 1837 Daguerre had developed a satisfactory process using silver plates. They were first polished and then made light sensitive by immersing them in iodine vapour. After exposure for about half an hour in a camera a latent image was formed in the silver iodide. This was revealed using the fumes of heated mercury and fixed by removing the unused silver iodide with a hot salt solution. The positive image produced by this process could then be viewed by holding the plate at such an angle

1

that the dark areas, represented by the polished silver, reflected no light while the light areas were formed by the silver mercury amalgam.

Daguerre's invention was announced to the world on 7 January 1839 and he was persuaded by a pension from the French Government to make it freely available to all – all, that is, except in England where he had patented his process on 14 August, five days before publishing the full details. John Goddard, who had been hired by Richard Beard to operate the process in his studio, discovered in 1840 that the addition of bromine to the iodine sensitising vapour improved the exposure time considerably. By 1841 it had been reduced to 20 seconds and by the next year to 10 seconds, making its use for portraiture practicable even though the sitter had to be kept still by a variety of clamps and props carefully kept out of view of the camera. Because of the care necessary in polishing the plate, sensitising it, developing the image and finally mounting it behind glass with an air tight seal, a daguerreotype was expensive – a portrait measuring 2½ by 2 inches cost a guinea. But it had another major disadvantage that was to lead to its early demise – each picture was unique and could not be reproduced; if more than one picture was required a new exposure at full cost had to be made – it was in fact a dead-end process which could not live with the very flexible system introduced by Fox Talbot.

In 1834 Fox Talbot began experimenting to find a method of recording the images of the *camera obscura* and by the next year he had succeeded – his process is described in chapter three – but did little further work on it until January 1839 when he was surprised by Daguerre's announcement of his discovery. Fox Talbot hastily arranged for Michael Faraday to display examples of his pictures to the Royal Institute on 25 January 1839 and himself read a paper *Some account of the art of Photogenic Drawing* to the Royal Society on 31 January, followed on 20 February by another giving details of his process – the prototype of the familiar negative-positive process. In 1841 he patented an improved process for producing what he was to call calotypes. The control he exerted over photography through this patent limited its use, especially

commercially, although he placed no restrictions on amateurs. It was not until he relinquished his rights in 1852 that it enjoyed a limited popularity. But by then new and better processes were appearing which replaced both the calotype and the daguerreotype.

It was, however, the calotype which Hill and Adamson used to record the first known views of York and with which William Pumphrey established the success of the first business in York solely concerned with photography. Fox Talbot followed Hill and Adamson to York and made some calotypes but by the time Roger Fenton arrived he was using Frederick Scott Archer's superior collodion process as also were George Washington Wilson and Francis Frith. George Fowler Jones, probably the first amateur photographer in York, started using the calotype in 1851 and continued using paper negatives, presumably because of their relative simplicity, until George Eastman introduced cellulose nitrate negatives in 1889. It is to these men that we are indebted for the early photographic record of the City. Their work can be readily identified. Additionally in the late 1850s photographic businesses started to appear in the City in increasing numbers and while mainly concentrating on portraiture they also took pictures of the streets and buildings which now cannot always be attributed to a particular firm or photographer.

This book is concerned with the photographs and photographers of the City from 1844 when the first pictures were taken to 1879 when the commercial availability of dry plates freed photographers from the necessity of making their own plates and carrying a portable darkroom, gave them a light sensitive emulsion that was capable of being manufactured with consistent characteristics, thus allowing exposures to be calculated beforehand rather than by trial and error and, by the great reduction in exposure times, made possible the photography of moving subjects. From this time, then, a new dimension was given to photography – to the 'still life' of architecture and portraiture was added the ability to record spontaneous action. The photographer could now take his camera into busy streets; no longer would he have to suffer the blurred or ghostly images of people moving during the relatively long exposures.

2 David Octavius Hill and Robert Adamson

YORK WAS THE BIRTHPLACE, IN 1831, of the British Association for the Advancement of Science. The idea for its formation came from Scotland, the proposal of David Brewster, an Edinburgh physicist, in an article the previous year in the *Quarterly Review*. He followed this with a letter to John Phillips, secretary of the Yorkshire Philosophical Society, asking if York, as the most central city in the three kingdoms, would be host to the inaugural meeting of the new association. York accepted and the meeting was held on 27 September 1831, organised by the Y.P.S. who also provided the principal officers of the B.A.

Sir David Brewster (he was knighted in 1831) was a close friend of Fox Talbot who sent him details of the calotype process in May 1841. By this time Brewster was principal of St. Andrew's University and he passed on the information to his professor of chemistry, Dr. John Adamson. Adamson, then, made the first calotypes in Scotland. Soon afterwards Fox Talbot, having been advised by Brewster that there would be no financial advantage in patenting the process in Scotland, filed his specification limiting his rights to England, Wales and the town of Berwick-upon-Tweed. He was, however, concerned that the daguerreotype was establishing itself in Scotland and asked Brewster if he knew anybody in that country who would be willing to use his process professionally. Brewster had the very man on his doorstep, John Adamson's younger brother, Robert, who, because of indifferent health, was having difficulty in finding a career. Robert, tutored by his brother, made his first calotypes in August 1842 and by July the next year

had set up his studio at Rock House, Calton Stairs in Edinburgh.

On 18 May 1843 Sir David Brewster, who had been ordained in 1804, was in Edinburgh attending the General Assembly of the Church of Scotland. Together with 154 other ministers he marched out of the meeting to form the Free Church of Scotland. Also present at the Assembly was David Octavius Hill, a landscape and portrait painter. He was so moved by the Disruption and subsequent events that he decided to paint a commemorative picture of the signing of the Act of Separation and Deed of Demission at Tanfield Hall. His aim was to produce an accurate likeness of all the 470 people present. The problems were enormous; not least how quickly to record the faces of all those involved. The answer came from Sir David Brewster. Hearing of Hill's predicament he showed him a calotype and sent him to see Robert Adamson who agreed to make the required portraits. From this meeting sprang a successful partnership which lasted until Adamson's death on 14 January 1848 at the age of 27. Their skills were complementary; Hill arranged the sitters and composed the picture and Adamson with the camera and chemical processes executed it. Between them they produced at least 1500 photographs bringing no return to Fox Talbot whose patent, after all, did not cover Scotland.

The final link in the chain which led to the taking of the earliest known photographs of York was forged, as all the others had been, by Sir David Brewster. He was by now a Vice President of the British Association and he suggested to Hill and Adamson that they should attend its 14th annual meeting, which was to be held in York in 1844, to record the participants. Fox Talbot's permission was needed for this venture, their only photographic excursion into England. Hill wrote to him on 21 September and such was the speed of the mails at the time that Fox Talbot's reply of 24 September with his agreement reached Hill at York on 28 September, having been redirected from Edinburgh. This was the third day of the conference, a day on which the Chemical Science section heard a paper on 'the Energiatype and the propriety of sulphate of iron in developing photographic images'. Professor William R. Grove detailed the experiments he had made on photographic paper but Fox Talbot when invited to address the meeting declined but promised to make some remarks at a future session.

On arrival Hill had set up his dark room and studio within the ruins of St. Mary's Abbey and by nightfall had made portraits of the Marquis of Northampton and the Earl of Inniskillen, both members of the B.A. establishment. By Monday, 30 September, Hill had had a notice printed inviting members of the B.A. to sit for him.

*Calotype Portraits of
Distinguished Members of the British
Association*

———

It has been considered desirable that the opportunity afforded by the present meeting should be embraced in order to secure Portraits in Calotype of the leading members of the Association.

Mr. Fox Talbot, the discoverer and patentee of the Calotype process has liberally given his permission, and the Local Committee have kindly afforded the necessary facilities at the Museum for carrying this design into execution.

. . . .

is respectfully requested to further the above object by sitting for his portrait, here, at any hour on Monday, Tuesday or Wednesday between the hours of nine and four o'clock. The sitting occupies only a minute or two.

Mr. D. O. Hill, R.S.A. will superintend the artistic arrangement of the sitters.

A few specimens of Messrs. Hill and Adamson's Calotype Pictures may be viewed at the Museum.

*York Museum
Monday, 30th September 1844*

Hill and Adamson, October 1844: Professor William Robert Grove (1811-96), a scientist attending the British Association meeting in a pose arranged by David Octavius Hill in the studio in St. Mary's Abbey. In his later years he became a judge of the Queen's bench.   National Galleries of Scotland

Although Robert Adamson is mentioned on this notice, there is some doubt about his presence at the conference. Certainly he is not included in the list of those who attended. Fox Talbot was invited to pose; if he did his portrait no longer exists but some 50 other calotypes made at York can be identified – of famous scientists and local Yorkshire dignitaries.

The Chemical Science section devoted a great part of their session on 1 October to photography. Robert Hunt read a paper on the amphytype, a process invented by Sir John Herschel. He was followed by Dr. Lyon Playfair who read Dr. Wood's paper on the electrolysotype and E. Solly presenting a paper on etching photographic plates by Dr. Hamel. Finally, fulfilling his previous promise, Fox Talbot made some extempore observations on photography, describing his own methods and objecting to all the new names that were being given to new processes – electrolysotype, tythonicity and energiatype etc. He pointed out the evils that would accrue to science if a new name was given to each development in photography.

On 4 October, two days after the conference was over and in the same week that the first daguerreotype studio opened in York, Hill and Adamson took their camera to Bishopthorpe Palace to complete their series of calotypes with a few studies of the Archbishop of York, Edward Venables Vernon Harcourt, and his wife. Their work at York consisted almost entirely of portraits – said to be not their best work – not because of any lack of the artistic expression which they were to so ably demonstrate was possible with the new medium, but rather the use of paper which had been prepared some time in advance instead of just before exposure. But it would have been surprising if they had been able to resist the photogenic possibilities of their surroundings. Two topographical pictures of York by them still exist, the earliest known of the buildings of the City. One shows the setting of their studio and darkroom, the ruins of St. Mary's Abbey, and the other the front of the south transept of the Minster with a group of top-hatted and frock-coated men in the doorway, possibly some of the distinguished scientists attending the B.A. Conference.

Soon after the death of his partner in 1848 David Octavius Hill gave up photography and returned to painting. He was, however, in 1858 elected a council member of the Photographic Society of Scotland. This had been founded in April 1856 by Sir David Brewster who was its first president. Hill died on 17 May 1870 aged 68, four years after the Disruption painting, which had brought about the famous partnership, was completed.

Photographs by David Octavius Hill and Robert Adamson

1. St. Mary's Abbey, Nave and N.W. Crossing Tower
   National Galleries of Scotland

2. York Minster, South Transept, Door and Clock
   National Museums of Scotland. Neg. No. 1377

Hill and Adamson, October 1844: The ruins of St. Mary's Abbey (N.E. corner of the nave), the site of their photographic studio during the British Association for the Advancement of Science meeting in 1844. *National Galleries of Scotland*

Hill and Adamson, October 1844: At the south door of the Minster a group of men who may be some of the distinguished scientists attending the British Association for the Advancement of Science meeting at the museum of the Yorkshire Philosophical Society in 1844 pose for the photographer. The slow speed of the photographic emulsions at this time is demonstrated by the transparent standing figure in the foreground, who has not been present for the full exposure, and the missing minute hand of the clock.

National Museums of Scotland

3 William Henry Fox Talbot

WHILE THE EARLIEST KNOWN photographs of York had been taken in 1844 using his calotype process, William Henry Fox Talbot did not himself bring his cameras to the City until the next year. In July 1845, accompanied by the Rev. Calvert Jones and Nicholaas Henneman, his ex-valet and now manager of his Reading photographic establishment, Fox Talbot set out on an excursion which included both York and Bristol. The purpose of the excursion was to give Jones instruction and experience in making calotypes before he went to the Continent later in the year. Their visit to the City is commemorated by 24 surviving pictures, not only the earliest series of views taken in York but also in Yorkshire. It must also have been the first opportunity the citizens had had of seeing photographers at work – Hill and Adamson, after all, had spent most of their time in the ruins of St. Mary's Abbey in the private grounds of the Yorkshire Philosophical Society. On 29 July Fox Talbot wrote to his wife 'We took twelve views of York today, most of them good. Crowds of admiring spectators surrounded the camera wherever we planted it.'

A record of these crowds would have been of great interest to present day historians but Fox Talbot, like all his contemporaries, used his cameras as a substitute for the artist's palette. They gave them the ability to produce a picture without acquiring or even being proficient in the practical skills of a painter in mixing colours and using a brush. He nevertheless applied the eye of the artist to the composition of his pictures. If people appeared they were carefully placed in ones or twos. An uncontrolled crowd would have been unwelcome in his pictures of buildings even if its members could have all kept still during the long exposures. The few pictures that Fox Talbot took of the streets of York are empty – giving the impression of a deserted city, but in reality they are a testament to the state of the photographic art at the time.

William Henry Fox Talbot had, in fact, started his photographic experiments over 11 years earlier in January 1834 because he was unable to make satisfactory sketches of the images cast in the *camera lucida*. He was born on 11 February 1800 at Melbury, Dorset, the home of his mother's family. His father's family had owned Lacock Abbey, Wiltshire, since 1544, albeit with the succession passing through the female line on three occasions, but William Davenport Talbot, an officer in the Dragoons, had been forced to let the Abbey to help settle the enormous debts his extravagance had brought him. William Davenport Talbot died only six months after the birth of his son who did not regain possession of the family home until he was 27. In the meantime young Fox Talbot was sent to boarding school, first at Rottingdean and then at Harrow, before going to Trinity College in Cambridge in 1817. He developed a wide range of intellectual interests which ranged from science to ancient history, from linguistics to fine arts. He had been made a member of the Royal Astronomical Society in 1822 and ten years later was elected to the Fellowship of the Royal Society. He had now been living at Lacock Abbey for five years and thus had a home in which to install his new wife, Constance Mundy of Markeaton, Derbyshire, who he married in December in the same year. Having in the same month become M.P. for Chippenham, Fox Talbot was unable to take a honeymoon until Autumn 1833 when the couple visited Italy. Early in October they were at Lake Como where he amused himself by taking sketches with a *camera lucida*.

He wrote later 'In honesty I should say attempting to take them but with the smallest possible amount of success. For when the eye was removed from the prism, in which all looked beautiful, I found that the faithless pencil had only left traces on the paper melancholy to behold. I then thought of trying again a method which I had tried many years before. This method was to take a *camera obscura* and to throw the image of the objects on a piece of transparent tracing paper laid on a pane of glass in the focus of the instrument. This led me to reflect on the inimitable beauty of the pictures of nature's painting, which the glass lens of the camera throws upon the paper in the focus – fairy pictures, creations of a moment, and destined as rapidly to fade away. It was during these thoughts that the idea occurred to me: how charming it would be if it were possible to cause these natural images to imprint themselves durably and remain fixed upon the paper! And why should it not be possible? I asked myself.' This desire to use the image of the *camera obscura* to 'draw' a permanent picture marks the inception of modern photography.

The Fox Talbots returned home early in 1834 and soon afterwards he started experimenting, first using the well known light sensitive properties of silver nitrate and then, because it was insufficiently sensitive, silver chloride. He formed this substance on a piece of paper by first coating it with a common salt solution and, when dry, with silver nitrate. When an object like a leaf or a piece of lace was placed on the treated paper, sunlight turned the uncovered areas black leaving a white silhouette. He noticed during the course of these experiments that in areas of the paper, particularly near the edges, the blackening effect was more rapid. This led him to the discovery that the sensitivity could be greatly increased by weakening the initial sodium chloride solution. But his images were still not fixed and the white outlines would gradually darken until the whole sheet of paper was uniformly black.

He then turned his attention to silver iodide because Sir Humphrey Davy had said it was more sensitive to light than silver chloride but to his surprise he found it 'absolutely insensitive to the strongest sunlight'. He realised, however, that he now had the means of fixing his images. If a picture made with silver chloride was dipped into a potassium iodide solution the light sensitive chloride was converted into insensitive silver iodide. He

was later to find that this process would cause his images to fade away in time but by February 1835 he had discovered that a boiling sodium chloride solution produced a greater degree of permanence. His images were, of course, white on a black background – negatives, as Sir John Herschel was to call them – but positives could easily be made by using the negatives as the primary objects to cover the sensitised paper.

Having now found a process which would record drawings made by light, Fox Talbot's next step was to try to achieve his original objective of imprinting the images of the *camera obscura*. The results were unsatisfactory; a two hour exposure produced only the outline of the building which the camera was directed at and the architectural details were feeble with those in the shade being left blank. More light was needed and he made a small camera which his wife was to call a mousetrap. This concentrated the image on to a very small area and coupled with improvements to the sensitivity of the paper enabled him to make a satisfactory negative with a ten minute exposure. The oldest known negative, of a latticed window in Lacock abbey, is dated August 1835.

With the basic objective achieved Fox Talbot virtually abandoned photography for three years – only to be shocked into new activity in January 1839 by Daguerre's announcement of his process. On 25 January Michael Faraday exhibited a number of Fox Talbot's 'photogenic drawings' to the Royal Institution which were greatly admired. Six days later Fox Talbot himself read a paper describing his process to the Royal Society. It was still not yet capable of capturing the fine detail of the daguerreotype which was now freely available except in England. Fox Talbot determined to perfect his process and in 1841 filed a patent for the calotype (Greek, kalos-beautiful) process. He treated paper with silver nitrate and then potassium nitrate. When this was dry it could be kept until required for exposure. At this time it was washed in a solution of silver nitrate, acetic acid and gallic acid which produced what he called gallo-nitrate of silver. After a short exposure in the camera no visible image could be seen but there was a latent image which could be revealed by washing the paper again with gallo-nitrate of silver and fixed in potassium bromide rather than the now familiar and superior 'hypo' – sodium thiosulphate – discovered by Herschel two years previously. He was however to include this in a further patent in 1843 in which he also mentioned a method of making the negative more translucent, which would improve the quality of the positive prints made from it, by waxing it.

The exploitation of this process was greatly stifled by Fox Talbot's requirement that anyone wishing to use it should be licensed by him. The first licence was issued to Henry Collen, a painter. This allowed him to practise professionally in London in exchange for 30% of his income – paid to Fox Talbot. Amateurs were treated more liberally; a fee of two guineas gave them the privilege of taking photographs for their own pleasure. Later they could obtain their licences freely if they purchased three guineas worth of iodised paper from the photographic establishment which Fox Talbot had set up, first in Reading and later in London, under the management of Nicholaas Henneman. Here pictures were printed from negatives and distributed for sale in shops, valuables and

antiques were photographed and their owners supplied with prints and anyone wanting to learn the new art could be given instruction at a price which included the licence fee. The initial objective was to make the plates for *The Pencil of Nature*, a book Fox Talbot published in six parts between June 1844 and April 1845 to demonstrate with pictures and text the superiority of the calotype over the daguerreotype in most areas of photography. Nevertheless photographers were deterred from using the process professionally by the licence requirements so it was never as popular as its rival which, with its sharp focus and attractive presentation case, proved ideal for portraiture – its main use. Fox Talbot relaxed his hold on calotypes in 1852 and allowed his patent rights to lapse altogether in 1854, shortly after a court case which established that he had no claim under his patents over Frederick Scott Archer's superior wet plate process. But however short lived was his process, Fox Talbot, who died on 17 September 1877, is justifiably called 'The Father of Modern Photography'.

Photographs by William Henry Fox Talbot

Taken July 1845	Science Museum Negative Number	Size (approx.) in inches
1. The Minster, south transept	357/69	7 × 5½
2. St. Mary's Abbey, nave (with Revd. Calvert Jones)	358/69	7 × 5½
3. The Minster, S.E.	359/69	7 × 5½
4. Kings Staithe	360/69	7 × 5½
5. St. Mary's Abbey, north east corner of nave	361/69	7 × 5½
6. St. Mary's Abbey, detail of nave north wall	362/69	7 × 5½
7. St. Mary's Abbey, nave (with ghost woman)	363/69	7 × 5½
8. The Minster, south transept, vestry and Zouche Chapel	364/69	7 × 5½
9. St. Mary's Abbey, west front	365/69	7 × 5½
10. Micklegate Bar	366/69	7 × 5½
11. St. Helen's Square	367/69	7 × 5½
12. Pavement	368/69	7 × 5½

Taken July 1845	Science Museum Negative Number	Size (approx.) in inches
13. The Minster, south door	369/69	5 × 4
14. The Minster, south transept	370/69	5 × 4
15. The Minster, door in south west tower	371/69	5 × 4
16. The Minster, south (with carriage and Revd. Calvert Jones)	372/69	5 × 4
17. The Minster, west door	373/69	5 × 4
18. Museum of Yorkshire Philosophical Society (with Revd. Calvert Jones)	374/79	5 × 4
19. Multangular Tower (with Revd. Calvert Jones)	375/69	5 × 4
20. Kings Staithe	376/69	5 × 4
21. The Minster, S.E.	377/69	5 × 4
22. The Minster, Chapter House	378/69	5 × 4
23. St. Mary's Abbey, detail of west front	379/69	5 × 4
24. The Minster from Lendal	2075/77	9 × 7

Fox Talbot, July 1845: At the south side of the Minster choir – to the left of the horse cab – stands the Reverend Calvert Jones who came to York with Fox Talbot in July 1845 to learn the art of photography. As he appears in many of the pictures taken by Fox Talbot on this visit one wonders how he was given the required instructions, nevertheless the surviving pictures of his continental journey testify to the success of the venture.

Trustees of the Science Museum, London. 372/69

11

Fox Talbot, July 1845: The south transept of the Minster was restored and remodelled between 1871 and 1880 by George Edmund Street, consulting architect to the Dean and Chapter 1868–81. On the south front he removed the clock and erected three symmetrical triangular gables. The four drum turrets over the clerestory and aisle walls were replaced by pinnacles and a heavy central pinnacle over the rose window, carrying the statue of a fiddler, gave way to a smaller and lighter cross. One consequence of this work was that the rebuilt clerestory walls were able to withstand the effects of the fire on 9 July 1984 and the major damage was confined to the roof. *Trustees of the Science Museum, London. 370/69*

Fox Talbot, July 1845: Before the buildings in the foreground on the corner of Blake Street and Lop Lane (Little Blake Street) were removed during the construction of Duncombe Place between 1860 and 1864, the west front of the Minster was largely obscured. A similar glimpse of the Minster, its splendour increased by the narrowness of the street, can today be found in Precentor's Court. On the extreme right of the picture is part of Ettridge's Hotel, rebuilt – as a Register Office in 1860.

Trustees of the Science Museum, London. 2075/77

13

Fox Talbot, July 1845: Calvert Jones is placed in front of the Multangular Tower to give interest and scale to what otherwise would be a very mundane picture of a structure which, though centuries old, has changed very little and in itself gives no clue to the date of the photograph.
Trustees of the Science Museum, London. 375/69

Fox Talbot, July 1845: The York Philosophical Society opened their new museum, designed by William Wilkins in the revived classical style, in 1830 to house their growing antiquarian, archaeological, geological and natural history collections. It was the birth place of the British Association for the Advancement of Science in 1831 to which it returned in 1844 for the meeting which brought Hill and Adamson to York. *Trustees of the Science Museum, London. 374/69*

Fox Talbot, July 1845: Calvert Jones stands against a wooden doorway leading from the ruins of St. Mary's Abbey into the graveyard of St. Olave's church. This is now occupied by the tomb of William Etty, R.A., a York born artist with a national reputation and a champion of the cause of preserving York's ancient buildings, who died on 23 November 1849.

Trustees of the Science Museum, London. 358/69

Fox Talbot, July 1845: The lantern tower of St. Helen's church was added in 1814 to replace a steeple which was in danger of falling down. The buildings on the right hand, part of Harker's hotel, were demolished in 1927 to enlarge St. Helen's Square, originally formed out of the churchyard in 1745 to improve the access to the Assembly Rooms in Blake Street. The top storey of the building on the corner of Stonegate, to the left of the church was removed shortly before the second world war.
Trustees of the Science Museum, London. 367/69

17

Fox Talbot, July 1845: Pavement seems unusually deserted. With the long exposures required at this time it would not have been possible to keep the crowds who normally thronged the streets still for long enough to prevent the picture being spoiled by blurred or ghostly images so the area must have been specially cleared for the photographers. St. Crux church was pulled down with the aid of dynamite in 1887, although the urns on the tower were removed a few years earlier. The jettied buildings on the right, then in an advanced state of disrepair, were demolished during the construction of Piccadilly in 1912.

Trustees of the Science Museum, London. 368/69

18

Fox Talbot, July 1845: In the centre of Kings Staithe is First Water Lane leading to a notorious slum area (partially cleared, together with the double gabled building in 1851). The notice board over the doorway of the Kings Arms, on the left of the Lane, proclaims that the landlord is Mr. Blundy. He took over the licence only three months before the picture was taken. The boats moored at the staithe are a reminder of the importance the Ouse once had as a trading artery, a role which it has not been able to sustain against competition, first, from the railways and later, from lorries and juggernauts.

Trustees of the Science Museum, London. 360/69

19

Fox Talbot, July 1845: The access through the main entrance to the City was gradually improved from 1753. In that year the additional arch on the left hand side of Micklegate Bar was constructed. Next in 1826 the barbican was removed followed in 1827 by the breaking through of the right hand side arch. St. Thomas' Hospital on the corner of Nunnery Lane was founded in the 14th century for the maintenance of the poor and to provide hospitality for travellers. It was pulled down in 1863 and replaced by a new building further down Nunnery Lane next to Victoria Bar (now the Moat Hotel).

Trustees of the Science Museum, London. 366/69

4 William Pumphrey

On the 14 July 1849 the *Yorkshire Gazette* announced that 'William Pumphrey having purchased of the former holder of the licence his sole right of taking photographic portraits in York and its vicinity begs to inform the public that every convenience for obtaining accurate and beautiful portraits will be found at his establishment at 51 Coney Street. Prices reduced one-half'. The last phrase suggests that Samuel Walker, an artist with premises at 50 Stonegate, by charging one guinea, had not successfully exploited his exclusive right to make daguerreotype portraits in the City which he had held since October 1844. Having sold his concession to Pumphrey he returned, for a short while, to conventional portraiture (one of his paintings, of Lieut. Ainslie of the 1st Royal Dragoons, was exhibited at Mr. Glaisby's Repository of Arts in Coney Street in March 1850) but in September 1850 he disposed of this business as well and left York for the U.S.A. where he died on 3 December 1872 at Salem, Virginia.

William Pumphrey was born on 4 February 1817, in Worcester, the eldest son of a Quaker glover, Joseph Pumphrey, and attended the Friends School at Thornbury, Gloucestershire before commencing business as a grocer in the town of his birth. After the failure of this enterprise he came to York and in 1845 became a science teacher at Bootham School during the headmastership of John Ford. At this time photography was emerging as a new art, or science, and it aroused Pumphrey's interest to such an extent that in 1849 he decided to leave teaching to start a Photographic Portrait Gallery in Coney Street. This was to be York's first business devoted entirely to photography.

When, on 30 July 1852, Fox Talbot offered all his patent rights, with the exception of portraiture, as a free present to the public to stimulate further improvements in photography, Pumphrey was then able to use the more flexible calotype process and started taking pictures of the streets and buildings of York. Six of his pictures are dated; the earliest, 4 October 1852, perhaps marking the commencement of the work which led to the eventual publication in 1853 of the earliest comprehensive photographic record of the streets and buildings of the City. The pictures were issued in serial parts and a cover with title page and introduction was available to house the complete portfolio of 60 views.

On the title page two lines by Longfellow set the scene:

> Quaint old town of toil and traffic,
>> quaint old town of art and song
> Memories haunt thy pointed gables,
>> like the rooks that round them throng.

Pumphrey's introduction explained that 'the views comprised in this series may be considered as illustrating the Antiquities of York under the heads of Military, Ecclesiastic and Civic and Domestic Edifices; to the first belong the Gates and City Walls that give to York some of its most striking peculiarities; to the second, its beautiful Minster and Monastic Ruins; whilst the last comprises such specimens as we have been able to give of the old gabled houses, etc., which are so fast disappearing from its Streets' – the last comment one which has been echoed time and time again by those concerned with conservation. Because topographical pictures were virtually unknown at this time, early photography having been mainly concerned with portraiture, Pumphrey found it necessary to say 'in conclusion it may not be amiss to state that as all photographs are monocular pictures they are seen to best advantage by looking at them with one eye only, when the effect of distance, (which it is often supposed that these pictures fail to give) is most faithfully rendered.'

The number of pictures in each of Pumphrey's three categories is:-

Military		19
Ecclesiastic	Minster & Dean's Park	11
	Abbeys, Priories, etc.	11
	Churches	8
Civic & Domestic		11
		60

and includes four pictures of buildings outside the City, two of Heslington Hall and one each of Bishopthorpe Palace and Skelton Church. While many of the pictures by the nature of their subjects are timeless, nevertheless there is sufficient in them to make them a valuable record of many past features of the City – of buildings that have vanished or changed significantly, of streetscapes that include road surfaces – cobbled paving, and lighting-gas, which have all long since disappeared. Some of the pictures unfortunately have faded with time and exposure to light, a common problem with calotype prints on salted paper, and many have a slight lack of sharpness due to the thickness and texture of the negative paper scattering the light during the contact printing process.

Other pictures by Pumphrey still exist – one, notably, of the river window of the Guildhall. This window now contains stained glass by Harry Harvey, giving a kaleidoscopic view of the City's history including the consequences of the bombing on 29 April 1942 – the fire which destroyed its predecessor installed in 1863 to commemorate Alderman James Meek, Lord Mayor in 1836, 1848 and 1850. Pumphrey's picture is therefore particularly valuable as it is the only record of the first stained glass in this window, installed in 1682 by the York glass painter, Henry Gyles. If it was taken shortly prior to its removal then it was after Pumphrey had disposed of his photographic business to George Brown in November 1854.

Pumphrey left commercial photography to become the superintendent of a private lunatic asylum in Lawrence House, Lawrence Street. He was, no doubt, influenced in this decision by his father-in-law, Thomas Allis, superintendent of the Retreat, whose daughter Elizabeth, he had married on 23 April 1851. But, in spite of this further change in his career, photography was not abandoned. For the rest of his life he took pictures on his travels both in England and abroad and made lantern slides of them for the enjoyment of his friends and family. While still in York he gave lectures on scientific subjects, not only to the boys of Bootham School but at the York Institute for Popular Science, Art and Literature, where the subject was sometimes photography. One such lecture on 7 November 1854 was, according to the *Yorkshire Gazette*, 'handled with great ability by Mr. Pumphrey. The lecturer entered at some length into the origin and progress of the art during the last 30 years and discussed the merits and demerits of the several processes, the daguerreotype and calotype. He illustrated his remarks with some interesting experiments and a large collection of very beautiful photographic pictures. The audience, a very numerous one, appeared to be highly pleased with this very instructive lecture'.

In 1866 Pumphrey, inspired by his visit to the Great Exhibition in 1851, organised, as joint secretary, a very successful exhibition of Yorkshire Fine Art and Industry in the grounds of Bootham Park Hospital. He also was an exhibitor himself, entering two revolving stereoscopes each containing 50 stereoscopic views. At the close his services were rewarded by the gift of a telescope and £100. The success of this exhibition encouraged him to organise a second in 1879. Another presentation, of a book case and library table, was made to him in 1881 at the Mansion House by Dean Purey Cust, on behalf of the citizens of York, on the occasion of his retirement to Bath where he served on the City Council and joined the Microscopic and Photographic Societies. On 28 March 1905, ten years after he had moved to Bristol, he died in his eighty-ninth year, still leading a life full of activity and still practising, now as a hobby, the subject which he had first taken up over half a century previously and which has assured for him a permanent place in the photographic history of York.

Photographs by William Pumphrey

Photographic Views of York and its environs			published 1853

1. Micklegate Bar from within   ES   234
2. Micklegate Bar from without   taken 9 October 1852
3. General view of the City   taken 4 October 1852   ES   333
4. Tower at Lendal Ferry   taken 6 October 1852   ES   424
   (west side)
5. Tower at Lendal Ferry   taken 8 October 1852   ES   423
   (east side)★
6. Bootham Bar from within
7. Bootham and Bootham Bar
8. Tower on the Esplanade
   (St. Mary's Abbey Water Tower)
9. Marygate Tower   ES   1484
10. Multangular Tower – interior
11. Multangular Tower – exterior
12. Monk Bar
13. City Walls near Layerthorpe Bridge   ES   849
14. The Red Tower   ES   391
15. City Walls near Walmgate Bar   ES   486
16. Walmgate Bar from within   ES   1800
17. Walmgate Bar from without
18. Fishergate Bar
19. Fishergate Postern
20. Cliffords Tower
21. Old Wharf, Skeldergate★   taken November 1853   ES   362
22. The Minster from Monk Bar
23. The Minster choir, eastern portion   ES   1499
24. The Minster, south transept   ES   1814
25. The Minster (S.E.) from the School of Design   ES   1813
26. The Minster from Museum Garden Gates   EN
27. The Minster, west doors
28. The Minster, north transept
29. The Minster, Chapter House
30. The Deanery
31. The Minster Library
32. Ruins of St. Mary's Abbey, the nave
33. Ruins of St. Mary's Abbey, eastern portion

Photographic Views of York and its environs			published 1853

34. Ruins of St. Mary's Abbey, western portion
35. St. Mary's Abbey – Marygate entrance
36. Hospitium of St. Mary's Abbey
37. Ruins of St. Mary's Abbey, Chapter House
38. St. Leonard's Hospital from Museum Street   ES   425
39. St. Leonard's Hospital from Museum Gardens
40. Priory Gateway, Micklegate   EN
41. Remains of St. George's   taken 6 October 1852   ES   346
    Priory (Castle Mills Bridge)★
42. St. Olave's Church
43. St. Helen's Church
44. St. Michael le Belfrey Church
45. Holy Trinity Church, Micklegate
46. St. Dennis' Church, Norman porch
47. St. Margaret's Church, Norman porch
48. St Lawrence's Church, Norman porch
49. Skelton Church – 3½ miles north of York
50. Doorway of Old Palace (Kings Manor)
51. The Guildhall from opposite bank of river★
52. The Guildhall, entrance
53. St. William's College
54. Old Houses in Pavement
55. Old Houses in Skeldergate
56. Old House on the (Kings) Staith
57. Old brick house, Clifton
58. Archbishop's Palace, Bishopthorpe – 3 miles from York
59. Heslington Hall, porch
60. Heslington Hall (east front) – 1½ miles from York

★ Several slightly different prints exist of some of the published pictures suggesting that Pumphrey made several negatives of each view.

Other photographs
   Guildhall, east (river) window

ES   Evelyn slide
EN   Evelyn negative

Pumphrey, 1853: Micklegate, at this time, was paved with cobbles and the Bar is surrounded by buildings all long since altered, replaced or, like the Jolly Bacchus public house on the right of the Bar, pulled down for street improvements in 1873 when the licence was transferred to 20 Melbourne Terrace. The tavern on the left is the Barefoot Inn which closed in 1928. Until 1827 the upper stories of the interior facade of Micklegate Bar were similar to those still surviving at Walmgate Bar. They were supported by a stone arch which carried the wall across the street. *Evelyn Collection*

Pumphrey, 6 October 1852: A passenger waits at Barker Tower on the west bank of the Ouse for the ferry to arrive at the landing at the bottom of the steps. It ceased to operate, after centuries of service to the citizens of York, on 8 January 1863 when Lendal Bridge was opened. The last ferryman, John Leeman, was compensated for his loss of employment by a public subscription which raised £40. On 13 May 1863 he was presented with a horse and cart and the balance of £15 in cash.

Evelyn Collection

Pumphrey, 8 October 1852: On the opposite side of the river a notice on Lendal Tower proclaims (indistinctly as the scattering of light in the paper negative has caused a slight loss of focus) that it is the office of the York New Waterworks company. The waterworks was established here in 1677 with its header tank in the tower. Water was pumped up, in turn by water wheel, horse gin and, finally, steam engine. With the Victorian population explosion a better water supply was necessary so a new waterworks was opened at Clifton Scope in 1849 but the offices remained here.

Evelyn Collection

Pumphrey, 1853: The tower built in 1829, when Layerthorpe postern was demolished, houses the workshop of an appropriately named cabinet maker, Thomas Walls. Widening of Layerthorpe bridge in 1929 necessitated the tower being rebuilt 12 yards further back. Farther along the wall a house can be seen, constructed on top of Harlot Hill tower, opposite a solitary dwelling, St. Maurice's House.

Evelyn Collection

Pumphrey, 1853: The City's defences between Layerthorpe postern and the Red Tower were completed by the fishpond of the Foss. The tower, probably built in 1490 may originally have stood on an island in the fishpond. By the 18th century it was in ruins and in 1853 can be seen to have been crudely rebuilt. It was given its present hipped tiled roof by George Fowler Jones during its restoration in 1857-8. To the right is the new building (1849/51) of the County Hospital. Its faintness is due to fading caused by the action of light on the salt print.

Evelyn Collection

Pumphrey, 1853: The small arch to the left of Walmgate Bar was constructed in 1804 and replaced in 1862 by one which was sufficiently large to allow the passage of electric trams when the Hull Road route was opened in 1916. Inside Walmgate Bar buildings line Walmgate right up to the walls. Next to the corner shop is the very narrow entrance into Waterhouse's Yard, one of the tenement lined courts which abounded in this area and provided substandard and insanitary homes for the poor. After the first world war the Corporation embarked on a programme of moving these people to new houses in the suburbs – but new communities have since been established in flats built after the second world war in the cleared areas.

Evelyn Collection

Pumphrey, 1853: Fishergate Bar was blocked in 1489 after damage by rebels and reopened in 1827 when the cattle market was moved outside the walls. The Phoenix Inn, originally the Labour in Vain, occupies the building whose chimneys can just be seen above the wall on the right hand side. The landlord, Meggeson Fields, has shown some enterprise in obtaining the right to place his sign where it could be seen by the farmers and dealers visiting the cattle market and hopefully tempt them away from the more convenient City Arms in Fawcett Street.

Pumphrey, 1853: Clifford's Tower with its motte curtailed and contained within a circular wall and on the right the Governor's house of the civil prison constructed between 1826 and 1835. In 1900 it was handed over to the military authorities who continued to use it as a prison until 1929. Five years later it was sold to the Corporation who demolished all its buildings, including the outer walls and gatehouse, in 1935. In the foreground can be seen the transparent image of one of the deer which were kept on the Eye of York – the grassed area in front of the Assize Court. It has only been in the picture for part of the long exposure.

Pumphrey, 4 Oct. 1852: The most popular view of the City taken by countless photographers, both amateur and professional. At this time the area alongside the walls is occupied by the coal drops and sidings of the York and North Midland Railway. In front of the Minster is the apsidal ended Lendal Chapel, built in 1816, and the skyline to the right is broken by the Mansion House which towers over the medieval Guildhall. In the right foreground are the houses of the now vanished streets on either side of Rougier Street – Albion Row, Providence Place, Simpson's Row, Queen Street and Calvert's Court.

Evelyn Collection

Pumphrey, 1853: To overcome the problem of converging parallels, caused by the unavoidable necessity to tilt the camera when photographing tall buildings, Pumphrey has raised his viewpoint as high as possible. He has taken his picture of the south aspect of the Minster from the roof of the School of Design built for St. Peter's School in 1833 and occupied by it until 1844 – now the Minster Song School whose grounds, marked by the iron railings in the foreground, were curtailed by the construction of Deangate in 1903. The heavy stone pinnacle surmounted by the little fiddler, at the southern extremity of the transept roof, was removed by G. E. Street during his alterations in 1871-80.   *Evelyn Collection*

Pumphrey, 1853: The angle of the walls of St. Mary's Abbey alongside Marygate and Bootham terminate in a round tower rising out of a foreground of cabbages and cold frames in the grounds of St. Mary's Abbey. The tall thin houses in Marygate on the left were removed in 1921 while the timber framed house built against the Bootham walls was pulled down and its site cleared in 1897.

Evelyn Collection

Pumphrey, 1853: The streetscape of Micklegate was changed in 1854 when the gateway to the Benedictine priory was removed along with the tenements that had been built in and around it. This demolition was to allow access to a new street, aptly named Priory Street, which eventually became one of the centres of non-conformity in York with the building of chapels for the Wesleyans (1854), Baptists (1868) and Presbyterians (1879).   *Evelyn Collection*

Pumphrey, 1853: Apart from the street lamp and the buildings behind it, this picture of St. Michael le Belfrey church could have been taken much more recently. The lamp was supplied with gas by the York United Gas Light Company, formed by the amalgamation of two competing companies in July 1844. The buildings behind it were pulled down between 1859 and 1864 during the widening of Lop Lane (Little Blake Street) and replaced by what is now the Dean Court Hotel.

Pumphrey, 1853: In photographing the west front of the Minster through Lop Lane (Little Blake Street), Pumphrey has taken his camera farther back than Fox Talbot and included in his picture the Lendal club and the entrance to St. Leonard's Place (constructed 1833/4) on the left and Ettridges (now Thomas's) Hotel on the right.

Evelyn Collection

Pumphrey, 1853: On the banks of the Foss next to the Castle Mills, until 1565, stood St. George's Chapel. Its stones were then used to repair Ouse Bridge which had been partially destroyed by floods. On its foundations a timber frame house was built – which eventually became the Windmill Inn. This was swept away in 1856 to create a basin in the river to improve the facilities for barges arriving at the Glass Works and those proceeding upstream to Leetham's Corn Mills and other businesses that lined the banks of the Foss.

Evelyn Collection

Pumphrey, 1853: These buildings in Skeldergate sit on the stone footings of the earlier medieval riverside. Apart from the Dutch gabled warehouse, unfortunately demolished in 1970, the others were replaced in 1873/4 by the Bonding warehouses built to encourage sea-going shipping to use the port of York. Above the house at the left is the cupola of the City Jail built 1802/7 and redundant by 1880 when it was pulled down.

Evelyn Collection

Pumphrey, 1853: In the eight years that have elapsed since Fox Talbot recorded the buildings on King's Staithe a change has been made. To the left of the Georgian facade of Cumberland House a new building, the Ship Inn, has appeared during the demolition of First Water Lane in 1851 to replace the twin gabled house. The houses on the right of Cumberland House were demolished by 1882 when the clearance of the Water Lanes was completed and the slums became just an unhappy memory.

Pumphrey, 1853: On the corner of Albion Street and Skeldergate, William Temperton sells provisions. His successor, William Henry Thomas, turned the shop into a beer house – eventually to spread into the timber framed building to the right and be named Plumbers Arms. The landlady between 1892 and 1927 was Mrs. Elizabeth Parks who was famous for her annual dinners for her friends and customers. The Plumbers Arms was demolished in 1964 and rebuilt as the Cock and Bottle but on a new building line well set back from the pavement edge.

5 Roger Fenton

IN THE AUTUMN OF 1854 a strange vehicle arrived in York accompanied by three men who, there, hired a horse to pull it on a journey to Rievaulx Abbey. The men were Roger Fenton, a photographer who was going the next year to the Crimea to take pictures of the war, and his assistants, Marcus Sparling and William. The vehicle was formerly a Canterbury wine merchant's van but Fenton had converted it into a travelling dark room and living accommodation. He had chosen Yorkshire for a trial trip because he thought it would most closely reproduce the conditions likely to be found in the Crimea.

He had been engaged for this venture by Thomas Agnew, the Manchester publisher, because of his proficiency with the new collodion process which he had adopted in 1853. This process, invented by Frederick Scott Archer, was announced to the public in March 1851. It had several advantages over the calotype; the glass base to the emulsion was clear and strong, the exposure time was short and it was proved not to infringe Fox Talbot's patents. However it had one major disadvantage. The glass plates were prepared by coating them with collodion (gun cotton dissolved in ether) and sensitising them with silver nitrate solution but to achieve the higher speed the plates had to be exposed in the camera while still wet and developed immediately afterwards. This meant that the photographer had to carry with him a portable darkroom, normally a tent, and glass plates and chemicals wherever he went.

The conditions in the Crimea demanded something more permanent and more readily available than a tent so Fenton devised his travelling dark room. After his return from the Crimea, with 360 pictures taken between February and June 1855, he described his van to the Photographic Society in January the next year. 'When it entered into the service of Art, a fresh top was made for it, so as to convert it into a dark-room; panes of yellow glass, with shutters, were fixed in the sides; a bed was constructed for it, which folded up into a very small space under the bench at the upper end; round the top were cisterns for distilled and for ordinary water, and a shelf for books. On the sides were places for fixing the gutta-percha baths, glass dippers, knives, forks and spoons. The kettles and cups hung from the roof. On the floor, under the trough for receiving waste water, was a frame with holes in it in which were fixed the heavier bottles. This frame had at night to be lifted up and placed on the working bench with the cameras, to make room for the bed, the furniture of which was, during the day, contained in a box under the driving seat.'

Roger Fenton, although for a period a full time professional photographer, was basically a lawyer. He was born in 1819, the fourth child of 17 presented to his father, John Fenton, a flannel manufacturer and banker of Rochdale, by his two wives. After gaining a degree at University College, London, Fenton studied art and painted, for a time in Paris where his interest in photography was aroused by the daguerreotype. Realising that art could never support him Fenton returned to London to study law, qualifying as a solicitor in 1847 and being called to the Bar four years later. During this time he started using the more flexible calotype process and in 1847 was a founder member of the Calotype Club. In *The Chemist* in March 1852 he proposed the formation of a national photographical society. On 20 January 1853 from this initial proposal the (Royal) Photographic Society emerged with Fenton as its first secretary. By 1854, while still shown in the law lists, he was engaged totally in photography; in that year he had been commissioned by

Queen Victoria and Prince Albert to take pictures of the Royal family and was appointed photographer to the British Museum. For both these assignments he used the collodion 'wet plate' process which was to lead to his journey to the Crimea.

The photographs he took on his trial trip were mainly architectural; of Rievaulx and Fountains Abbey and, at the start of the journey, York Minster where he chose the southern aspect already recorded by Fox Talbot and Pumphrey. At this time a clear view of the west front, so beloved of photographers today, was blocked by the buildings lining Lop Lane (Little Blake Street) – now Duncombe Place – so Fenton had to content himself, as had his predecessors, with a photograph from Museum Street to capture what could be seen of the Minster over the buildings in between and along the narrow lane. He also took two pictures of the west door from different view points. Some of his photographs taken at this time were published and were sold to the public, perhaps to raise money to help pay for the trial. One of these, a picture of Lendal Ferry and the river Ouse is dated 1 October 1854, indicating by the speed with which it was produced that publication was planned in advance of the trip. Fenton's York photographs show between them his artist's eye for composition, his mastery of technical problems like converging parallels and the superior clarity and sharpness of the wet plate process over the calotype.

In August 1856 Fenton joined the Photo-Galvanographic Company on a part time basis as manager of its photographic department and chief photographer at its premises in Islington. This company had been set up to publish photo engravings using the process patented by an Austrian, Paul Pretsch, first in 1854 and with improvements in 1855. From a print made from the original negative a copper plate was eventually produced by photographic, chemical and electrical means which carried the original image but with the detail raised in relief. After a certain amount of hand retouching to recapture any fine detail which had been lost in the various stages of the process, this plate was used in a printing press to produce the 'engravings'. Using this process the company published in October and put on sale in December 1856 part one of *Photographic Art Treasures* which contained four prints of Fenton's own photographs including one entitled 'York Minster from Lendall [sic]', a picture which he had taken on his pre-Crimean trial trip. As only some 500 prints could be made from the copper plate, which deteriorated progressively, the prints were sold as choice proofs at 10s. 6d., proofs at 7s. 6d. and ordinary prints at 5s. 0d. Fenton's association with the company ended in late 1857 or early 1858 when, due to its low sales, it was wound up.

Fenton was involved from 1859 with another publisher, Lovell Reeve of Covent Garden. Their *Stereoscope Magazine* was entirely devoted to stereoscopy, the production of a three dimensional image from two photographs of the same view taken from the same distance apart as the human eyes. Wheatstone's reflecting stereoscope was first offered for sale in 1846 but the popularity of this aspect of photography had to wait until 1851 when Sir David Brewster's two lens box type instrument was displayed at the Great Exhibition. Finally in 1861 the popular stereoscope appeared, invented by Oliver Wendell Holmes, the American anatomist and author, who suffered from headaches when using the box type for any length of time. Fenton's involvement with stereoscopy started very early in his photographic career and his pictures regularly appeared in the magazine. The issue for August 1860 contained a most unlikely view for the stereoscope; his picture of the west door of the Minster has insufficient relief to exploit properly the full potential of this branch of photography.

On 15 October 1862 Fenton announced to the public his intention to give up photography completely. His reasons for this are unknown. His equipment was sold at auction on 11 and 12 November and he returned to the Law until his death, aged 49, on 8 August 1869.

Photographs by Roger Fenton

1. Lendal Ferry	published 1 Oct. 1854		
2. York Minster from S.E.	taken on		
3. York Minster, west door	pre-Crimean	ES	1812
4. York Minster, west door and railings	trial trip Sept./Oct. 1854	ES	529
5. York Minster from Lendal	published Oct. 1856	ES	266
6. York Minster west door	Stereoscopic view published Aug. 1860		

Fenton, September 1854 – published 1 October 1854: The steps of the ferry landing have provided a vantage point for this picture entitled Lendall [sic] Ferry. The gentleman in the stove pipe hat, perhaps a friend of Fenton, is obviously out of place amongst the planks and baskets on a working boat. Beyond the moored commercial vessels are rowing boats available for hire from William Hill who, in April 1845, had taken over the tenancy of the ferry from John Brown. After the opening of Lendal Bridge and the closure of the ferry in January 1863 the Hill family continued to run the boat yard until 1 November 1971 when the last member retired.

Fenton, September 1854: The eye is led into the picture by the carefully placed figure who stands on the steps of the west door of the Minster looking at the work of William Shout (1751 – 1826), Master of the Works for the Dean and Chapter. Between 1802 and 1816 Shout carried out a complete restoration of the west end with the help of the York sculptor, Michael Taylor (1760 – 1846), who carved the statues of Percy and Vavasour, donors of materials for the Minster in the 14th century.

Evelyn Collection

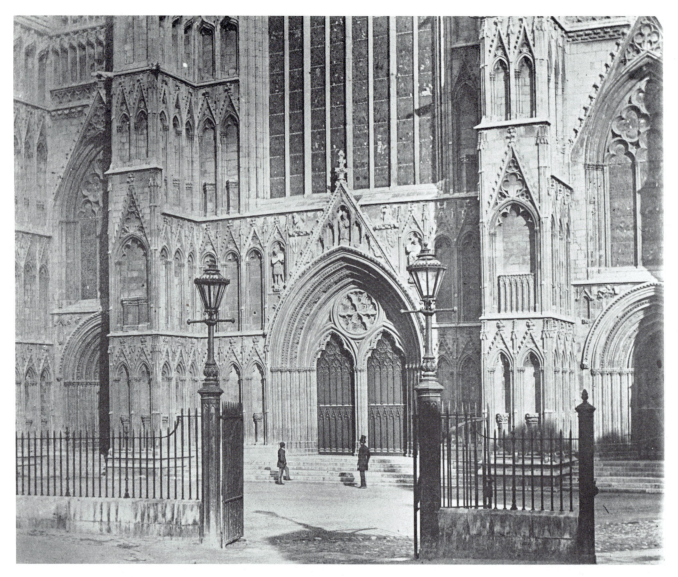

Fenton, September 1854: In a second picture, taken at the same time Fenton has framed the west door of the Minster with the lamp posts on either side of the gateway in the iron railings of the Close. These were supplied in 1839 by John Walker from his foundry in Walmgate and removed to their present position on the boundary of Deans Park in 1863 during the construction of Duncombe Place. With the almost complete extinction of gas street lighting the lamps have been skilfully converted to electricity using small bulbs similar in appearance to the incandescent gas mantles they have replaced.

Evelyn Collection

Fenton, September 1854 – published October 1856: Like Fox Talbot and Pumphrey before him Fenton thought that the glimpse of the west front of the Minster through Lop Lane (Little Blake Street) would make a good composition. That his picture appears to have an unnatural sharpness is due to the photo-galvanographic process which allowed the plates from which the reproductions were made to be touched up by an engraver before printing. *Evelyn Collection*

6 George Washington Wilson

In 1852, FOUR YEARS after the famous Scottish photographic partnership of Hill and Adamson ended with the premature death of Robert Adamson, a studio was opened in Crown Street, Aberdeen where the sitters could have their portraits made either by photography or by painting. These alternatives were offered by George Washington Wilson, an artist, who realised the adverse effect the new science could have on his livelihood. From this small beginning grew a business that was known world wide for the quality of its topographical photographs – a reputation based on the artistic talents and technical abilities of its founder.

George Washington Wilson was born on or about 7 February 1823 at his father's croft near Banff. George Wilson and Elspet Herd were eventually to produce 11 children and it seems probable that they gave their second son the additional name of Washington as a tribute to the first president of the U.S.A. At the age of 12 young George left his school at Forglen to start an apprenticeship with a carpenter and housebuilder, an apprenticeship that was to last for 11 years until 1846. A talent for painting and drawing took him, shortly afterwards, to Edinburgh to get a formal education in these subjects before moving to Aberdeen. A short sojourn there was followed in 1849 by a visit to London and Paris to gain more experience. On his return to Aberdeen he set himself up as an artist and teacher of drawing and painting. While portraiture was his main occupation, he produced, in 1850, a detailed bird's eye view of the topography of Aberdeen, a complicated exercise in changing perspective from his ground level observations to an imagined position above the City. (A similar feat for the City of York was undertaken by Nathaniel Whittock in 1858.)

It is not known where Wilson gained his knowledge of photography. He was certainly in Edinburgh while Hill and Adamson were practising from their Calton Stairs studio and it would seem he was well aware of the limitations of the paper based calotype process in recording fine detail. It is, therefore, significant that Wilson's professional adoption of photography happened only a year after Scott Archer announced to the public his invention of the glass based collodion process. Despite the complications of this process (see chapter 5), its ability to produce sharp negatives with short exposure times must have appealed to Wilson who could then produce portraits of a quality approaching daguerreotypes but with the added advantage that multiple copies could easily be produced.

The ceremony on 23 September 1853 at which Queen Victoria laid the foundation stone of her new highland castle at Balmoral also symbolised for Wilson the foundation of his own success and prosperity. The previous year Prince Albert had asked him, perhaps on the recommendation of his Aberdeen architect, William Smith, to record the progress of the building which was to replace the older and smaller original castle. This first royal commission was the start of a long professional association for Wilson with the Queen and allowed him, although without official authority, to advertise that his firm was 'Under the Immediate Patronage of Her Majesty', and later 'Photographer to the Queen'. 20 years elapsed before he applied to the Lord Chamberlain for a royal warrant and not until 17 July 1873 was he properly entitled to call himself 'Photographer to Her Majesty in Scotland' – by special appointment.

But Queen Victoria's selection of Scotland for her summer home benefited Wilson in another way; her example was followed by others, not only those who could afford to buy or build residences there but by an ever increasing number of tourists attracted by the beauty of the Scottish scenery, brought to their attention, partly at least, by the Queen's choice. Wilson responded to the increase in tourism by providing photographic mementoes of the landscape, particularly in the form of well composed views for the stereoscope, which in the late 1850's was at the height of its popularity. Stereographs were selling at this time for two shillings each and he published his first list of them in 1856 – all Scottish subjects. In 1860 he made a photographic foray into England – London and the south coast – followed by another the next year when he went as far as Cornwall. During this period he added architecture to his portfolio, a collection of exteriors and interiors of English Cathedrals. Wilson's 1863 list included 13 stereographs of York Minster, all taken the previous year. They were later reissued as album views, 3⅛ × 4¼ in. pictures, which were printed from one half of a stereograph negative. Some of these were used in 1865 to illustrate *York and Durham* one of a series of booklets he published under the general title of *Photographs of English and Scottish Scenery*, each containing 12 plates.

In these early days, Wilson submitted examples of his work to photographic journals for review, presumably a device to obtain free publicity, provided, of course, that the reviewers liked his work which they invariably did. Four of his York photographs were thought worthy of a mention by the *British Journal of Photography*. On 2 February 1863 it was said that 'The Interior of the Lantern Tower' should be viewed 'with the stereoscope held up towards the ceiling, so as to look upwards as if viewing the original, otherwise the reality of the appearance is lost'. Of the three stereographs reviewed on 9 December 1864 it was thought that the view of the Minster from the south east was least interesting. Every photographer prior to 1862 recorded this view, as at the time, it was the only aspect of the Minster not in part obstructed by other buildings. The other two pictures were of the west front; one showing the doorway with the effigies of Percy and Vavasour over it was very fine while the other had 'the new Roman Catholic Chapel of St. Wilfrid on the left, seeming by its foreign style to flout the grand old building in whose shadow it may be said to lie'. With this picture Wilson was probably the first photographer to take advantage of the demolition of narrow Lop Lane (Little Blake Street) which made way for the new wide Duncombe Place. Wide angle lenses were not available to these early photographers and the full height of the west front of the Minster could only be recorded with the camera sited as far back as Museum Street and in that position it was previously partially masked by the now demolished buildings.

The granting of a royal warrant marked a new phase in Wilson's business which had to expand to meet the demands which success brought. He could no longer take all the photographs himself and had to rely on other freelance or staff photographers but, from whatever source, all the published photographs appeared under the trade mark GWW. In 1888 he retired and relinquished control to his three sons. His health was not good as he was suffering from fits perhaps induced by many years of inhaling ether fumes, a necessary but unfortunate concomitant of working in a confined space with collodion. After his death on 9 March 1893, after a particularly massive fit, his firm continued on in various guises until 1908 when it was wound up, the victim of the changing fashions and particularly the advent of the cheap and ubiquitous picture postcard which took the place of landscape photographs. Two York stationers published postcards which carried the GWW mark – Gray & Co. of Fossgate and Arthur & Co. of Davygate. The negatives from which these were made belong to the latter years of the firm and it would appear that one of the devices adopted in an attempt to halt its decline was permitting use of its negatives under licence to firms throughout the country to make postcards of their own locality.

Photographs by George Washington Wilson

Stereographs taken 1862	G W W Number	Listed in G W W Catalogues	Aberdeen University Library Negative No.[*2]
1. York Minster from Monk Bar (from N.E.)	364	a	F4389
2. York Minster from S.E.	365	a	F840
3. York Minster from W.	366 [*1]	a	F1839
4. York Minster from W.	366a [*1]	b	F1839X & F4395
5. York Minster, west door	367 [*1]	a	F4390
6. York Minster, south door	368	a	F4260
7. York Minster, nave looking west	369	a	F4386
8. York Minster, nave looking east	370	a	F2242
9. York Minster, choir looking west	371	a	F718
10. York Minster, choir looking east	372	a	F723
11. York Minster, the 'Five Sisters'	373	a	F1858
12. York Minster, the stone screen (and organ)	374	a	F1859
13. York Minster, the stone screen	375	c	F1860X
14. York Minster, interior of lantern tower	376	a	
15. York Minster, De Grey's monument	378	a	F1861

Stereographs taken before 1877	G W W Number	Listed in G W W Catalogues	Aberdeen University Library Negative No.[*2]
16. York Minster, Chapter House	606	b	F3399
17. St. Wilfrid's Church, west front	607	b	F1548
18. St. Wilfrid's Church, west door	608	b	F1326

Cabinet Picture taken before 1877			
19. York Minster from south	59	d	F897

a 1863, 1877 and 1893
b 1877 and 1893
c not listed in any catalogue
d 1877

[*1] two different views known to exist

[*2] In many cases more than one negative exists

1863 *List of Stereoscopic and Album Views*

1877 *Catalogue of Imperial, Cabinet and Carte-de-Visite Views*

1893 *Catalogue of Landscape and Architectural Stereoscopic Photographs*

While it is known that Wilson visited York in 1862 to make stereographs, it is not always certain that the negatives in the Aberdeen University Collection were made at this time. Some of the popular views were rephotographed later, but the negatives were given the same number, regardless of the date of photographing.

Wilson, 1862 (Stereograph 366a): This nationally known photographer from Aberdeen visited York when the houses on the city side of Lop Lane were being demolished during the making of a widened street to give better access to the railway station for the citizens who lived on the north east of the City. The cab, with its door open, has obviously just discharged its passenger but rather than wait until it had gone, Wilson has chosen to include it to enhance his composition by providing an object to lead the eye into the picture.
George Washington Wilson Collection, Aberdeen University Library

YORKMINSTER. WEST FRONT. 366. G.W.W.

Wilson, 1862 (Stereograph 366): The removal of the buildings which had once stood on the right hand side of Lop Lane allowed photographers, for the first time, an unobstructed view of the west front and nave of the Minster and Wilson was probably the first to take advantage of it. The new widened street was called Duncombe Place in honour of Dean Augustus Duncombe, who suggested the 'improvement' to the Corporation in 1859, shortly after his arrival in York.

George Washington Wilson Collection, Aberdeen University Library

Wilson, May 1865 (Stereograph 607): While one side of Lop Lane (Little Blake Street) was being demolished, St. Wilfrid's Church was being built (1862-4) on the other, replacing a small chapel, behind the theatre, which had served the Roman Catholic community since 1760. The gateway, framed by two gas lamps on stone pillars, was the entrance to the Theatre Royal until it was given a new front in St. Leonard's Place in 1835. *George Washington Wilson Collection, Aberdeen University Library*

Wilson, 1862 (Stereograph 364): Normally the necessity for anyone photographing the Minster to keep at a distance from it, thereby avoiding the converging parallels produced by tilting the camera, led to a large expanse of dull foreground. By taking his camera to the top of Monk Bar Wilson has overcome this problem and produced a much more interesting picture with the Minster rising out of the random pattern of the roofs and chimneys of Ogleforth, College Street and St. William's College.
George Washington Wilson Collection,
Aberdeen University Library

Wilson, 1862 (Stereograph 370): Inside the Minster Wilson found the nave furnished with only a few backless benches on each side which cannot have been sufficient or adequate for worshippers. The empty floor, however, enhances the majesty of the building. The shields in the spandrels of the arcade and in the central tower had been, since the fire of 1840, if not earlier, colour washed with lime and ochre. They were not given their appropriate heraldic tinctures until the 1930s.

George Washington Wilson Collection,
Aberdeen University Library

Wilson, 1862 (Stereograph 374): By avoiding the temptation of putting his camera symmetrically in front of the choir screen, Wilson has enlivened his picture by allowing a glimpse past the organ of the ribs of the roof of the choir, restored after the fire of 1829. The organ, also rebuilt at that time, had proved to be unsatisfactory and was completely reconstructed and renovated in 1859 when the protruding fan tuba (removed in 1903) was provided.

George Washington Wilson Collection,
Aberdeen University Library

Wilson, 1862 (Stereograph 371): The emptiness of the nave in a previous picture is explained by the many extra benches crowded in between the choir stalls and at the top of the steps in front of the high altar. All the services held in the Minster must have been confined to the choir. The heavy stone altar rails designed by Sir Robert Smirke in the 1829-32 restoration were later replaced with lighter wrought iron and after being re-used for a short time in the Lady Chapel disappeared finally earlier this century.

George Washington Wilson Collection,
Aberdeen University Library

7 Francis Frith

LIKE WILLIAM PUMPHREY BEFORE HIM, Francis Frith was a Quaker who started his first commercial venture as a grocer. He was born in 1822 in Chesterfield where his father was a cooper. Here he received his early education and developed a talent for painting and drawing. At the age of 12 he was sent to Camp Hill, a Quaker school in Birmingham which he left in 1838 to become apprenticed to William Hargreaves, a cutler. A nervous breakdown in 1843 led him, on medical advice to travel, to embark, with his parents, on a two year tour of Britain which must have awakened in him the ambition he was to realise in later years, the making of a complete photographic record of the picturesque scenery and buildings of the British Isles.

But first, his health restored, he began a wholesale grocery business in Liverpool which occupied him until 1850 when he decided to change to printing. When he became interested in photography is not known but he must have been aware of the emergence of the new science in 1839 and the work of the pioneers, Daguerre, Fox Talbot and Scott Archer. Certainly by 1853 he was one of the founder members of Liverpool Photographic Society and in 1856 was exhibiting portraits in London. This was the year he decided to sell his printing business and start a new one to take advantage of the growing interest in photography and, especially, the use of photographs to illustrate travel books. He bought a country house in Surrey, settled his parents there and then set off on the first of several photographic journeys he made over the next four years to Egypt, Palestine and Syria. The conditions he experienced there, working in his small dark-room tent in temperatures sometimes high enough to make the collodion boil when he poured it on the glass plates, as well as the difficulties of transporting all the paraphernalia required by early photographers must have served as an excellent apprenticeship for his subsequent

work in Britain. Seven books of photographs were the tangible result of this period of his career.

In 1860 Francis Frith married a fellow Quaker, Mary Ann Rosling and moved to Reigate where he founded the photographic business, F. Frith & Co., that was to enable him to commence his great ambition. He could not, of course, achieve this on his own and had to employ assistants who he trained in his own meticulous techniques of painterly composition. This ensured not only a high picture quality but the impossibility of determining which was his work. The firm made prints, sold singly or in albums, and stereographs. Some pictures are signed or embossed with, variously, his name, F. F. & Co. or Frith's Series; others are anonymous or the mount has a label 'Frith's Photo-pictures' attached. It is probable that only the pictures with his name were taken by Frith himself on the photographic trips he made by train to a convenient centre and thence by pony and trap to explore the locality. Frith, in the early years of his company, also published photographs taken by Francis Bedford, George Washington Wilson and, after buying his negatives in 1862, by Roger Fenton.

The pictures of F. Frith & Co., sold by hundreds of shops throughout the country, were available either mounted or unmounted in five sizes at prices ranging from 6d. to 2s. 6d. Each negative, when made, was allocated a sequential number which was used to identify the picture in the firm's catalogues. These numbers also enable the photographs to be dated reasonably accurately when they do not contain details that, after research, would reveal the required information. It is therefore possible to determine from a picture of York Minster from the south-east, numbered 278, that Frith or one of his assistants had visited York in 1861 showing that the firm had given high priority to the inclusion of the City in their photographic record.

The serial numbers also show that many visits were made to York to increase and update the views available for sale. Advertisements of 1880 and 1884 both announce that an 'entirely new series' of Frith's photographs of York had been made of all the well known streets and buildings of the City. They also reveal, perhaps surprisingly, that on at least 15 occasions during the lifetime of Francis Frith either he or his staff had been seen with their cameras and equipment out and about in the streets of York. The range of numbers are:-

2--	1861	98--	1877	187--	1886★
12--	1864	103--	1879	287--	1891
14--	1865	129--	1881	288--	1891
18--	1867	183--	1885	306--	1892★
34--	1871	184--	1885★	320--	1892
54--	1873	185--	1885	394--	1895

★ firmly dated from other evidence

Francis Frith died in Cannes 1898, four years after the Post Office made the first relaxation of its monopoly on the printing and stamping of postcards. On 1 September 1894 private postcards of official size (4¾ × 3 ins) could be sent through the post bearing a halfpenny adhesive stamp but their popularity was not assured until 1 November 1899 when full Postal Union size (5½ × 3½ ins) was allowed. F. Frith & Co. now under the management of Eustace and Cyril, two of the founder's five sons, were well prepared to take advantage of this removal of restrictions. Picture postcards were printed in their thousands from the invaluable stock of glass negatives, of views recorded years previously, particularly in 1885. Apart from their serial number, it is almost impossible to know that these had not been made currently, so skilfully were small anachronistic details removed. Photographers from the firm made at least six more visits to York between 1907 and 1925 (numbers 586-- to 789--) to ensure that the postcards offered for sale included contemporary views of the City showing major changes that could not be added to earlier pictures by retouching.

The firm closed in 1972 with nearly 60,000 glass plate negatives still stored at Reigate. While these have been preserved it appears that many of the early ones have not survived. Commercial considerations must have required that they were destroyed to make way for the rapidly expanding stock of later views. However valuable they would have been as a contemporary record, F. Frith & Co. could not afford the space to store any negatives no longer needed for the continued success of the business.

Early Photographs by F. Frith & Co.

		Probable date
	York Minster, choir looking east	
	York Minster, west door (F. Bedford, Phot.)	
278	York Minster, S.E.	1861
1281	York Minster, S.W.	1864
1283	York Minster, choir looking east (interior)	1864
1284	York Minster, choir looking west (interior)	1864
1285	York Minster, nave looking east (interior)	1864
1286	York Minster, nave looking west (interior)	1864
1290	York Minster, De Grey monument	1864
1418	York Minster, choir looking east (interior)	1865
1433	York Minster, choir looking west (interior)	1865
1854	York Minster, Chapter House (interior)	1867
3432	York Minster, N.W.	1871
3433	York Minster, E.	1871
3439	York Minster, north transept (interior)	1871
3440	York Minster, Chapter House (interior)	1871
3442	Walmgate Bar (interior)	1871
5413	York Minster, N.	1873

		Probable date
5445	Shambles	1873
54--	St. Helen's Square	1873
9855	York Minster, south choir aisle looking west	1877
10376	York Minster, choir looking west (interior)	1879
12902	York Minster, choir screen	1881
12911	York Minster, Lady Chapel (interior)	1881
12913	York Minster, Lady Chapel (interior) from west	1881
12915	York Minster, south choir aisle looking east	1881
12921	Walmgate Bar (interior)	1881
12930	Shambles	1881
12931	Lendal Bridge	1881
12935	York Minster from River Ouse	1881
12942	St. Mary's Abbey, S.E.	1881
12945	St. Mary's Abbey, E.	1881
12947	St. Mary's Abbey, Lady Chapel	1881
12948	St. Mary's Abbey and St. Olave's Church	1881
12963	Railway Station, train shed (interior)	1881

Francis Frith (3433), 1871: Having shortly after his appointment in 1858 personally subscribed £1000 towards the widening of Lop Lane (Little Blake Street) which improved the perspective of the west front of the Minster Dean Augustus Duncombe next had two houses at the east end demolished creating College Green. The Green was further extended in 1955 and the road connection from College Street to the south of the Minster was severed in 1972 when Queen's Path was made. The inadequacy of the medieval foundations is revealed by the vertical crack in the centre of the great east window. This appears to have been only recently repointed.

P. W. Hanstock

Francis Frith (54--), 1873: While Frith has entitled this photograph 'St. Helen's Church' he has, in fact, provided a view of the whole of St. Helen's Square. On the left is the shop of Stephen Davis, furrier, eventually taken over by Joseph Terry and Sons whose original shop is just off the picture. This is followed by the Grecian building of the Savings Bank (1829-30). In between Stonegate and the church, Frederick Holgate has a fancy repository. On the right an Irish linen warehouse is under the proprietorship of Martha, widow of James Magean who had commenced business in Petergate. He died in 1861 and his widow moved here in 1867 and finally, by 1881, to Coney Street.

Francis Frith (5445), 1873: Apart from James Pierce, a clothes dealer who moved to The Shambles from Patrick Pool c. 1866, all the other shopkeepers are butchers – the traditional trade of this street for many centuries. While there is now only one butcher in The Shambles to remind us of its origins there were 25 in 1872 out of 39 shopkeepers there. In 1280, almost 600 years previously, 17 butchers paid an annual schamel toll of 70 shillings between them.

Francis Frith (12930), 1881: Butchering was apparently a thirst making trade as there were four public houses in The Shambles at this time. The signs of The Neptune (closed 1903) and The Shoulder of Mutton (closed 1898) can be seen on the left, brought into the picture by the changed view-point chosen by the photographer on this later visit. Further down the street on the same side was a third public house, The Eagle and Child (closed 1925) and at the far end on the opposite side a fourth, The Globe (closed 1936). While there is only one butcher's shop to be seen there is no lessening in their numbers – the others have not yet laid out their meat on the benches.

Francis Frith (12963), 1881: In the 1860s George Hudson's dead end station inside the walls was handling, with great difficulty, over 100 trains daily. A better station with through running north to south was clearly required. Although the NER obtained an Act of Parliament in 1866 work did not start on the site outside the walls until 1873. The new station opened for traffic on 25 June 1877. With its magnificent cast iron train shed it surely ranks with the great Victorian railway termini described by John Betjeman as 'the cathedrals of the railway age'. Until 1900, when the footbridge was built, passengers had to cross the line by subways and the platforms gained their present numbers in 1938. The gas lighting gave way to electricity briefly from December 1881 to November 1882 when the gas was restored.   *Evelyn Collection*

Francis Frith (12931), 1881: Until 7 August 1894 anyone wishing to cross Lendal Bridge had to pay a toll to collectors in the toll-houses at each end of the bridge. These toll-houses were designed by George Page, the son of the bridge's designer, Thomas Page, and himself the designer of Skeldergate bridge. They were built by a local man, sculptor George Walker Milburn. The angels at the centre of the bridge arch were sculpted by a Mr. Tweedy of Newcastle from a photograph of the Princess of Wales, Princess Alexandra of Denmark. The likeness was said to be 'in every respect remarkable'. The bank of the river in the foreground was not piled, walled and sloped until 1914.

Evelyn Collection

8 *George Fowler Jones*

THE PHOTOGRAPHERS CONSIDERED so far were, for a time at least, professionals who made money out of the newly emerging art; Fox Talbot set up his Reading establishment to make calotypes and sell prints, an activity undertaken by Hill and Adamson in Scotland; Pumphrey for four years sold portraits and views to the citizens of York while Fenton's earnings came from a variety of photographic appointments and commissions and Frith and Wilson were entirely professionals. George Fowler Jones in these terms was an amateur but he used his camera over a period of at least 53 years as an adjunct to his chosen profession.

He was born in Aberdeen in 1819. His father, John Lloyd Jones, was a major in the Madras army. After his early schooling young Fowler Jones entered the office of William Wilkins, junior, an architect with a national reputation who had built the Yorkshire Philosophical Society's Museum (1827-9) in the revived classical style. Wilkins died in 1839 and his pupil transferred to another well known architect, Sydney Smirke. Smirke, too, worked in York, reinstating the nave of the Minster which was seriously damaged by fire on 20 May 1840, followed, when this was finished four years later, by the restoration of the interior of the Chapter House.

George Fowler Jones could not have worked in the City with Wilkins but he must have assisted Smirke with his work at the Minster. Thus familiar with York he decided, in 1846, to establish his own architectural practice there, at first at 51 Monkgate and later successively in New Street, Stonegate, Micklegate and Lendal. He was responsible for St. Thomas's Church, 1853/4; Clifton Church, 1866/7; Heworth Church, 1868/9; and Museum Gardens Gates and Lodge, 1874; and his alterations and restorations include St. John's, Micklegate, 1850; Red Tower, 1857; Unitarian Chapel, St. Saviourgate, 1860; St. Michael Le Belfrey Church, 1867 and St. Olave's Church, 1887/9. According to John Hutchinson (*York*: 1980) 'His Gothic is coarse, occasionally fun; certainly individualistic'. Fowler Jones died on 1 March 1905, having been assisted in his architectural practice in his latter years by Gascoigne, his son by his first wife.

During the whole time he practised in York he took photographs to record not only his own work but historic and picturesque buildings both in the City and throughout the country. His earliest pictures are dated 1851, a time when few people had embraced the new art, and the latest, 1904, when it was available to all. Over this period he must have taken many pictures but his positively known work is now represented by 64 negatives of York views and 60 prints of buildings in England and Scotland. Nearly all these negatives and prints are signed with a monogram of his initials, G.F.J. Strangely from those that are dated (63), it appears that his photography fell into three main periods – 1851-3, 1867-70 and 1881-7, the prints being almost entirely contained in the last period. The impression is given that Fowler Jones neglected photography during the intervening periods but no real conclusion can be drawn from such a small number of pictures.

With only two exceptions all George Fowler Jones' surviving York pictures are of buildings – as one would perhaps expect of an architect. Like his photographic contemporaries he selected the Minster (19 views) as his principal subject, surpassing even his record of his own buildings (15). St. Mary's Abbey (6) is well represented and the remainder mainly picture well-known buildings that have changed only little in the intervening years. It is not surprising that early exponents of the new art chose to photograph the antiquities of York rather than busy street scenes that would have been much more valuable to historians. They were using the new invention as an extension of art and naturally chose views that made the best compositions. Uncontrolled people and vehicles were not required; only an occasional carefully placed figure to give a focal point or scale. In addition to the principal buildings of the City and his own work, Fowler Jones photographed 84 (now 78) Bootham (where he lived from 1862 until he moved to Quarry Bank, Malton in the early 1870s) as well as Burton [Stone] Lane Windmill and Clifton Cottage – two long vanished structures. But despite the immutability of York's historic buildings, the views do portray many changes – the churchyard of St. John's, Micklegate, the rebuilding of the northern pinnacle tower at the east end of the Minster in 1853, the Museum Gardens bank of the Ouse before it was formalised, the rural surroundings of Clifton Church and a host of minor details. Fowler Jones' pictures, then, are an important record of the City's face in the infancy of photography, starting at the same time as the better known pioneers of photography but continuing long after they had gone from the City.

His negatives, as well as providing a means of reproducing the pictures, also show the development of the science of photography. The first ten, dated 1851-3, belong to the period when photographers themselves sensitised ordinary paper just prior to exposing it in the camera. The sheets had to be carefully selected to avoid watermarks. To avoid this problem manufacturers produced paper specially for photographers with these marks right at the edge. Fowler Jones used cartridge paper for his early negatives watermarked 'Photographic RT. . . .' and 'Chafford Mills'. On two of them (nos. 5 and 6) he has written his exposure times, 3 and 5 seconds, showing the slowness of the photographic process at the time. A further problem was the thickness and grain of the paper which, despite waxing it after development, scattered the light during the contact printing of the positive, resulting in a lack of sharpness.

A thinner more translucent paper was essential. The next series of negatives from the period 1863-70 shows this transition – to a pre-waxed tracing paper, sold under the name of 'Ceroline', that could be sensitised many days before exposure. This process, invented by Gustave Le Gray in 1851 was the culmination of the calotype, extending its life, particularly among amateurs who did not want to be cluttered by the paraphernalia that had to be taken on photographic excursions when using the superior wet plate collodion process.

The third group of negatives comprises five dated between 1885-7, one dated 1895 and five undated. They have been made on negative paper which was introduced by George Eastman in 1884. Glass plates, supporting a gelatine emulsion, had been commercially available since 1879, freeing the users of wet plates from the tyranny of carrying their dark room everywhere with them. By substituting paper for the glass plate Eastman sacrificed some print quality but removed the major disadvantages of glass – its weight and fragility. He was able to regain the loss of quality in 1889 by using transparent cellulose nitrate instead of paper. Fowler Jones' last six negatives are of this latter type and, while undated, must have been taken after that year.

In addition to his 64 surviving negatives of York views the subjects of another 25 of his pictures of the City are known. Between 15 March and 12 April 1905 an exhibition of *Old York Views and Worthies* was held in the Art Gallery. It was organised by George Benson, the architect and historian, and Dr. W. A. Evelyn at the inspiration of the latter to bring together as many pictorial representations of Old York as were known to be available. While the majority of exhibits were paintings, drawings or engravings a small number of photographs were also included. Gascoigne Hastings Fowler Jones, George's son, born in 1850, and a member of the organising committee, is shown in the catalogue as having entered 25 of his father's pictures, 20 of them taken in 1853. As George Fowler Jones died on 1 March, only 14 days before the exhibition opened, it is probable that he had helped in their selection, aiming at complementing the earlier work of artists and the contemporary photographs of William Pumphrey with views of the streets and buildings of York in the middle of the nineteenth century and also including some buildings which had vanished or streetscapes which had changed more recently. Only three titles can be recognised amongst the surviving negatives but a further eight may possibly be identified from otherwise anonymous photographs.

An unexpected use of photography is revealed in a book published in 1878 by G[ascoigne] H[astings] Fowler Jones. It is entitled *Sketches in York* and on the title page it is explained that the 50 drawings are 'from sketches made on the spot and Old Drawings, etc. still existing'. When Fox Talbot published the first instalment *The Pencil of Nature* in 1844 he included a pasted-in note which read 'Notice to the reader. The plates of the present work are impressed by the agency of light alone, without any aid whatever from the artist's pencil. They are sun pictures themselves, and not, as some persons have imagined, engravings in imitation.' It may be the sun's pencil that Gascoigne had in mind as the maker of the sketches on the spot for three of the drawings in the book have been traced from his father's negatives or the contact prints made from them. The two images fit exactly, the only difference being the omission of unimportant detail in the finished drawing. It is probable, then, that many of the other 47 drawings were made by the same method; further evidence that George Fowler Jones' photographic output was not limited to the surviving negatives and prints, the only vestiges of the work of York's first known amateur photographer.

Photographs by George Fowler Jones

Negatives in the Evelyn collection	Taken	Negative type and size
1. St. Leonard's Hospital	1851	a x
2. Multangular Tower	1851	a x
3. Monk Bar	1851	a x
4. Guildhall	20 Apr. 1852	a x
5. Clifton Cottage	18 Feb. 1853	a x
6. At Clifton Cottage	18 Feb. 1853	a x
7. Waterworks Tower and Guildhall	1853	a x
8. Minster, N.E. and Grays Court, from Lord Mayors Walk	1853	a x
9. Minster, N.E., from Lord Mayors Walk	1853	a x
10. Minster, E. end	1853	a w
11. St. Mary's Abbey, N.W. crossing pier from nave	May 1863	b z
12. St. Mary's Abbey, nave, interior	1863	b z
13. Clifton Church, S.E.	Oct. 1867	b y
14. Clifton Church, S.W.	Oct. 1867	b y
15. Clifton Church, E.	Oct. 1867	b y
16. Clifton Church, porch	Oct. 1867	b y
17. Revd. Metcalf's house, Haxby Rd.	Oct. 1867	b y
18. Kings Manor from Museum Gardens	Oct. 1867	b y
19. Clifton Church, S.	1868	b z
20. Clifton Church, N.	1868	b z

Negatives in the Evelyn collection	Taken	Negative type and size
21. Clifton Church, N.E.	1868	b z
22. Burton Lane Mill (side)　(2)	May 1870	b z
23. Burton Lane Mill (rear)	May 1870	b z
24. Monk Bar Walls	May 1870	b z
25. Minster, nave and W. towers, from Deans Park　(2)	July 1870	b z
26. Heworth Vicarage	Sept. 1870	b z
27. Heworth Vicarage	Sept. 1870	b z
28. Heworth Church, S.E.	Sept. 1870	b z
29. Heworth Church, E. end	Sept. 1870	b z
30. St. Mary's Abbey, from St. Olave's churchyard　(2)	1870	b z
31. St. Mary's Abbey, N.W. crossing pier	Undated	b z
32. St. Mary's Abbey, N.W. crossing pier and nave	Undated	b z
33. St. Mary's Abbey, W.	Undated	b z
34. Minster, W. towers from Old Residence　(2)	Undated	b y
35. Minster, S.	Undated	b y
36. North Street Postern	Undated	b y
37. St. Thomas's Church　(2)	Undated	b y
38. St. John's Church, Micklegate	Undated	b y
39. Heworth Church and Vicarage	Undated	b z

Negatives in the Evelyn collection		Taken	Negative type and size
40. Minster from Museum Street	(pre. 1863)	Undated	b y
41. Bootham Park	(after 1862)	Undated	b y
42. 84 Bootham	(after 1862)	Undated	b z
43. Minster, N. transept and Chapter House		1885	c x
44. Holy Trinity, Micklegate, tower		1886	c x
45. Marygate Landing and Manor Shore		1886	c x
46. Minster, N.E., from Grays Court garden (choir and central tower)		1887	c x
47. Minster, N.E., from Grays Court garden (choir, central tower and Chapter House)		1887	c x
48. Minster, E. end		1895	c z
49. Minster, S. (choir and central tower)		Undated	c z
50. Minster, N. and Old Residence		Undated	c z
51. Minster, E. end and St. Williams College		Undated	c z
52. Minster, nave and W. towers from Deans Park		Undated	c z
53. Minster, W. towers		Undated	c z
54. Minster, E. end and St. William's College	(After 1889)	Undated	d z
55. Minster, W. tower from Old Residence	(After 1889)	Undated	d z
56. Minster, nave and W. towers from Deans Park	(After 1889)	Undated	d z
57. All Saints, Pavement, E.	(After 1889)	Undated	d y
58. Petergate	(After 1889)	Undated	d y
59. Old Houses	(After 1889)	Undated	d y

Negative Type	Size (approx.) in inches
a. Coarse grained cartridge paper watermarked 'photographic RT. . .' or 'Chafford Mills'	w 5¼ × 6½
b. 'Ceroline' – waxed tracing paper	x 6½ × 8½
c. Eastman negative paper (introduced in 1884)	y 7 × 9
d. Cellulose nitrate (patented Dec. 1889 by Eastman)	z 8 × 10

Photographs taken by George Fowler Jones included in the Old York Views and Worthies Exhibition 1905

Catalogue Number	Title	Taken	Probable Identification	
955	The Trinity Priory Gardens	1853		
956	York from the Manor Shore	1853	FJN	7
957	Micklegate with Trinity Priory Gateway	1853		
958	Trinity Priory Gateway from the Priory Gardens	1853	ES	298
959	Micklegate Bar from Micklegate	1853		
960	Micklegate Bar from Blossom Street	1853		
961	Tanners Moat	1853		
962	Coney Street	1853	ES	2381
969	Old Crane, Skeldergate	1853		
970	North Street Postern	1853	ES	2380
971	Plummers Cottage, Clifton	1853		
972	Plummers Cottage, Clifton	1853		
973	Cottage, Water End, Clifton	1853	FJN	5
974	Plummers Cottage, Clifton	1853		
975	Water Tower, Lendal	1853	ES	660
976	Marygate Postern	1853		
981	Little Blake Street	1853		
982	Record Tower, Marygate	1853	ES	1886
983	Stonegate	1853	ES	2382
984	Bootham Bar from Petergate	1853	ES	2376
994	In Tanner Row	—		
995	The Record Tower, Bootham from Bearpark's Garden	—		
998	The Wheatsheaf Inn, Davygate, removed 1899	—	ES	911
999	Old Windmill, Burton Stone Lane	May 1870	FJN	22
1183	Entrance to Lendal before the present Post Office was erected [1887]	—		

ES Evelyn Slide

FJN Fowler Jones Negative

Fowler Jones, 1851: The thick cartridge paper of Fowler Jones' earlier negatives produces a distinct lack of sharpness. He too occasionally uses a solitary figure to add scale and harmony to his composition. Without this person and the pile of rubble on which he sits, the third century multangular tower would be virtually timeless. *Evelyn Collection*

Fowler Jones, 1851: The wall of the churchyard of the medieval church of St. Maurice has made an effective viewpoint for Fowler Jones to avoid the problem of converging parallels in his picture of Monk Bar. The two shops on the right were casualties to the remorseless advance of the internal combustion engine. They were pulled down in the early 1970s to make a straight connection between Lord Mayor's Walk and St. Maurice's Road. The small arch to the left of the Bar was enlarged in 1861.

Evelyn Collection

Fowler Jones, 1853: It was restoration work at the Minster which first introduced George Fowler Jones, as a pupil of Sydney Smirke, to York and led him to setting up his own architectural practice in the City in 1846. Here at the east end of the Minster he has recorded, on a negative made from a page torn out of his sketch pad, the reconstruction of the northern pinnacle tower.

Evelyn Collection

Fowler Jones, 18 February 1853: The caption *Clifton Cottage* written on the negative of this picture is of little help in identifying its location as there were, at the time, at least three other Clifton Cottages, all still in existence. The decrepit state of this one, particularly its roof, must mean that its days were numbered. Fowler Jones has also recorded that his exposure for this difficult snow scene was three minutes.

Evelyn Collection

Fowler Jones, 18 February 1853: An even longer exposure, five minutes, was used to record the farm buildings and implements behind Clifton Cottage. The weather must have stopped all the farm work but the compacted snow clinging to the wheels of the wagon on the left shows that it has been recently used.
Evelyn Collection

Fowler Jones, 1853: Ten years before Lendal Bridge was opened an unrestricted view of the buildings on the right bank of the Ouse, from Lendal Tower to Ouse Bridge, could be obtained from the Manor Shore (now The Esplanade). The river is contained by the remains of medieval buildings interrupted by the openings of lanes which led from landing places up to Coney Street. At the right is the end of a terrace of houses called Waterloo Place (demolished 1925) overshadowed by the tall buildings of Low Ousegate.   *Evelyn Collection*

Fowler Jones, 20 April 1852: The 15th century riverside frontage of the Guildhall was built over Common Hall Lane which then emerged under the arch on to the staithe. The extension to the right was made in 1810 to replace the old Council Chamber on Ouse Bridge, pulled down during the construction of the new bridge. No further changes were made until 1891 when a very much larger Council Chamber and municipal offices were added on the left.

Evelyn Collection

Clifton, York -

Fowler Jones, October 1867: The first proposal to build a church for Clifton was made in 1859 but six years later, despite a generous response to an appeal for funds, nothing had happened. In 1865, after rejecting a proposal to convert the chapel of St. Peter's School into a parish church, the Archbishop of York directed that a new church should be built. The foundation stone was laid in January 1866 and the building, designed by Fowler Jones and standing in very rural surroundings, was consecrated on 10 May 1867.

Evelyn Collection

Burton Lane York

Fowler Jones, May 1870: The existence of a windmill on this site in Burton Stone Lane was recorded in 1374 in the ownership of John de Rouclyff. Corn was still being ground there 500 years later but by the end of the nineteenth century the windmill had disappeared. This photograph with one other by Fowler Jones and two drawings traced from it by Gascoigne Fowler Jones and E. Ridsdale Tate are the sole reminders of the existence of the mill.
Evelyn Collection

Fowler Jones, May 1870: The house on Harlot Hill tower in the walls between Monk Bar and Layerthorpe postern was removed in 1877/8 during a restoration of this section of the walls when pepper pot bartizans were added to the tower and its parapet and platform were raised two feet. The tower of St. Cuthbert's church at the extreme left, deceivingly appears to be outside the walls, which, hidden by the ramparts swing to the left in front of it.

Evelyn Collection

Fowler Jones, no date: This picture, probably taken in the 1860s, in looking along the ruins of the nave of St. Mary's Abbey has as its central feature the N.W. pier of the crossing. Hill and Adamson in 1844 recorded it from the opposite side. What is now left of the Abbey helps to give us some impression of the magnificence of what was once one of the richest and most splendid of English Benedictine houses, surrendered to the King in 1539 to become a stone quarry for the builders in the City.

Evelyn Collection

Fowler Jones, no date: Until narrow Lop Lane (Little Blake Street) was widened between 1860 and 1864 to make Duncombe Place, unobstructed views of the west front of the Minster were impossible to obtain. By taking his camera to the roof of the New Residence, Fowler Jones has nearly succeeded. The buildings in the foreground were cleared away during the construction of the Purey Cust Nursing Home (opened 1919).

Evelyn Collection

Fowler Jones, 1860 or before: While his photographic predecessors stayed at ground level to take their pictures of the west front of the Minster framed by Lop Lane (Little Blake Street), Fowler Jones once again has gone to the roof tops. His picture, including additionally the central tower and south transept, taken from the roof of the Lendal Club emphasises the narrowness of Lop Lane and the dominance of the Minster over all other buildings in the City. *Evelyn Collection*

Fowler Jones, 1860 or before: With his architect's eye for composition, Fowler Jones has framed the Hospitium or Guest House of St. Mary's Abbey in the enlarged arch of North Street postern. The Hospitium was very much rebuilt 1930/1 when the upper storey was continued for the length of the building and it was given a steeper pitched roof. The postern was enlarged in 1840 by the Great North of England Railway to allow their carts to reach the coal sidings outside the wall. The £500 the Corporation received for granting the railway company this privilege was used to restore Walmgate Bar and its barbican.

Evelyn Collection

Fowler Jones, no date: in 1850 St. John's church in Micklegate was shortened from six to five bays to allow North Street at the right to be widened. At the same time a porch was added and the whole church was restored under the guidance of Fowler Jones. The churchyard was removed when Micklegate was widened in the 1960s and the pavement was laid right up to the walls of the church, now an Arts Centre, having last been used for worship in 1934.   *Evelyn Collection*

Fowler Jones, c. 1862: For about 10 years from 1862 George Fowler Jones and his family lived at 84 (now 78) Bootham. From an upper floor he had an uninterrupted view across the grounds of Bootham Park Hospital over the railings erected in 1857 by William Walker. The double fence on the left defines the line of the York and North Midland's railway to Scarborough which opened in 1845 and crossed Bootham in a cutting. In the fields beyond the railway Grosvenor Terrace was built c. 1880 followed later by Scarborough Terrace and Filey Terrace. *Evelyn Collection*

Probably Fowler Jones, 1853: In July 1848 John Glaisby purchased William Hargrove's bookshop and library and opened his Repository of Arts in Coney Street in a building which, since 1877 has been a newspaper office. In that year Glaisby moved to new premises in Spurriergate, taking with him his son William Punderson Glaisby, a professional photographer, who had started his business here. He would have been too young to have taken this photograph which predates the renewal of the church clock bracket in 1856.

Evelyn Collection

Probably Fowler Jones, 1853: The arrow slits, to enable the military to shoot arrows inwards at the citizens they are supposed to be defending, look out from Bootham Bar along High Petergate. They were erroneously added by Peter Robinson during a restoration in 1834. The remaining jettied houses have, in recent years, been stripped of their plaster, pandering to the current fashion of exposing timber framing. Richard Ealand, gas fitter, whitesmith and house bell hanger died in July 1866 when his business was taken over by Matthew Yarker, a plumber and glazier.   Evelyn Collection

Probably Fowler Jones, 1853: The familiar signboard of the Star Inn, crossing Stonegate, proclaims, in letters cramped into the space of an obviously shorter name, that the landlord's name is [Frank] Wheatley who was the tenant from 1853 to June 1856. By January 1857 he was an insolvent debtor. Next to Bellerby's Public Library was the shop of Thomas Lorimer, a fishmonger, one of two in the street at that time – a far cry from the present china and glass showrooms of Mulberry Hall.

Evelyn Collection

Probably Fowler Jones, 1853: The line of the inner arch of the Priory gateway in Micklegate can be seen just to the left of the steps leading to the tenements on the upper floor above those created by walling in the arch itself. All was demolished in 1854 to create Priory Street; yet another step in the relentless progress of what Dr. W. A. Evelyn, a pioneer of conservation, was to call in later years 'ruthless commercialism' which swept away York's heritage when it stood in its path.

Evelyn Collection

Probably Fowler Jones, 1853: Except for Marygate corner tower itself the walls of St. Mary's Abbey in Bootham are totally obscured by houses. Clearance was started in 1896 by the Yorkshire Philosophical Society who at that time owned the walls. Then the house immediately to the left of the tower was demolished and its site along with another further to the left, adjacent to the White Horse hotel, was cleared. Further clearances were made in 1914 and shortly after the second world war, but now with escalating prices of property more are unlikely.

Evelyn Collection

9 York Photographers

THE FIRST COMMERCIAL PHOTOGRAPHER in the City was Samuel Walker, a portrait painter. In October 1844 he announced to the 'inhabitants of York and surrounding District' that the daguerreotype process was being used to take likenesses at the photographic portrait gallery at 50 Stonegate, previously his studio, where he was in attendance between nine and five o'clock daily. There, for one guinea which included a neat morocco case, a customer could have his 'features admirably delineated' and take away a portrait in which 'every line, every touch in the picture produced is from the pencil of nature, without flattery or fallacy'. After persevering with this process for four years Walker returned to portrait painting and transferred his exclusive rights to take daguerreotypes in York and for 20 miles around to William Pumphrey.

In July 1849 Pumphrey opened the first exclusively photographic business in the City at 51 Coney Street and immediately reduced the price of a portrait by one half. As soon as Fox Talbot's calotype process was freely available for all photography except portraiture, Pumphrey used it to make a record of the City. From his original paper negatives he was able to make many prints which he offered for sale in sets in 1853 (see Chapter 4). Commercial photography only held him, like Samuel Walker before him, for four years and by the end of 1854 his business was taken over by George Brown who found the shop in Coney Street inadequate. He moved to premises at 3 Railway Street, where, according to his advertisement in the *Yorkshire Gazette* on 18 November 1854, 'having been built especially for photographic purposes G.B. can assure his Friends that nothing has been omitted which can in any way conduce either to their convenience or to the successful prosecution of the business'. In his new photographic portrait and apparatus rooms George Brown, who had also taken over the daguerreotype portraiture licence, sold equipment and gave instruction in every department of photography and made 'portraits for the stereoscope or ordinary' which were 'taken daily without regard to weather' and coloured 'by his new process'. He too found it necessary to reduce the price of daguerreotypes by a half – to five shillings but three years later he appears to have abandoned this process totally – in favour of Fox Talbot's more versatile invention. He revealed in February 1857 that he had secured, at great expense, the services of a miniature artist who would use his skills to colour calotype portraits thereby combining 'the beauty of the miniature painting with the truth of the photograph'. On his death in November 1862 the business was continued until 1887 by his brother-in-law, Robert Place who, in the latter years, also traded as a tobacconist.

By 1855 a second photographic business was started by Joseph Bryar, a chemist, in his shop at 39 Clarence Street. This was very shortlived but in the next three years another nine opened to compete with George Brown in offering the new and increasingly popular art to the citizens of York. One firm, W. T. & R. Gowland, at first in Ogleforth and from 1867 in Lendal, lasted over 100 years, finally closing in June 1963, albeit with three changes of proprietor – Edwin Pink in 1900, Harry Lane Smith by 1905 and finally Herbert Speed from 1924. The business was started by W. T. Gowland alone who offered to the public 'large and unique photographic portraits coloured in oil', which, he claimed, were very superior pictures combining the 'fidelity of the photograph with the artistic effect and durability of a first rate oil painting'. He was, however, 'prepared to take photographic likenesses of every style and size in a superior manner and at moderate prices'. Some time after this advertisement had appeared in the *Yorkshire Gazette* (7 May 1858) he took his brother, Robert, a house painter, gilder, decorator and japanner into partnership.

Surprisingly, the name of John Ward Knowles appears amongst these early photographers. He was born in 1838, the son of George Knowles, a plumber, glazier and house and sign painter in Goodramgate. His artistic talents led him away from his father's trade, first to photography and then, by 1861, to stained glass, an art in which he was to establish a local and to a small extent a national reputation. Later his studio was in Stonegate where he lived from 1874 to his death in 1931. At the same time William Bellerby, who in 1845 founded the painting and decorating firm still in existence as Bellerbys Ltd., advertised that, by letters patent, he was a photographer on cloth. At Walker's Photographic Rooms at 27 Davygate York citizens could, in 1858, get first class coloured portraits, equal to miniatures on ivory, at prices ranging from 2s. 6d. to £2. All these early photographers, of course, did their own processing and they could be supplied with Ramsden's emulsions and chemicals of guaranteed purity as well as transparent varnish requiring no heat by John Spurr, a chemist, trading from the Medical Hall in Goodramgate.

By the end of the period under consideration, 1879, the names of 34 photographers had appeared in the street directories; the maximum number practising at one time was 17 in 1872 but the average was 12. The bulk of their work was portraiture, made available to everybody through the medium of the carte de visite. In the early 1850s a large portrait cost two pounds or more, well out of reach of all but the more affluent. A few years later this was changed by the introduction of a small picture stuck on to a card, which measured 4 inches by 2½ inches, slightly larger than the visiting card which gave it its name, although there is no evidence of this use. In November 1861 W. T. & R. Gowland advertised that 6 cartes de visite, taken from life, would cost 10s. 6d. or 12 for 14s. 6d. while in November H. F. Newell at his City and County Cartes de Visite Portrait Rooms in Stonegate could provide 25 for one guinea. At the end of the century the price, generally, had fallen to 5s. a dozen. Its cheapness assured its rapid gain in popularity with many new businesses opening to satisfy the demands of the public. Not all the photographers had the time or even the

talent to inject any originality into their portraits but nevertheless reaped good rewards for their enterprise.

Many of these cartes still exist, both loose and in ornate albums made specially to house them. Unfortunately the portraits are of little value as the sitters are rarely identified. This was not thought necessary by their immediate relatives but two or three generations later it was too late and thus, devoid of family interest, the cartes were often discarded or sold cheaply to dealers in ephemera. The reverse of the card usually advertised the name and address of the photographer and his services, thus giving them a significance to local historians – even to the extent of providing evidence of photographers who appeared and disappeared in the time between issues of street directories. But in addition to portraiture cartes were occasionally used, before the advent of the picture postcard to provide pictorial souvenirs of their visits for tourists and of local events for residents. Photographs in newspapers, made possible by the invention of the half tone block in 1883, were rare before 1904 so the cartes de visite in capturing transitory moments in the life of the City are, where they still exist, a more valuable and accurate record than the engravings which were all the journalists had available to illustrate their articles.

As William Pumphrey was one of the organising secretaries of the Yorkshire Fine Art and Industrial Exhibition in 1866 it was only to be expected that photography would be included amongst the Fine Arts on display in the temporary building erected in the grounds of Bootham Park Hospital. Six York photographers, W. P. Glaisby, W. T. & R. Gowland, W. Monkhouse, H. F. Newell, W. Pumphrey and R. Wright, exhibited examples of their work and four of them gained awards. A medal, the most prestigious prize, was awarded to W. T. & R. Gowland for excellence in the production of both plain and coloured portraits and to W. Monkhouse for photographs of interiors. William Monkhouse came to York in c. 1838 and started a lithography business, the first in York. After some years he left the running of this firm to his assistants and worked with William Pumphrey, who was then practising as a professional photographer. Eventually Monkhouse decided to set up a second business as a photographer in Lendal and according to J. W. Knowles 'pursued photography with some ardour –

journeys were made in search of views and much fatigue had to be endured in the days when the wet process was the only one adopted but as new processes came up he was ever ready to adopt them'. He was the official photographer for the exhibition (producing a portfolio of views of the building and its interior) and, in addition to his medal, gained a certificate for ingenuity in the construction and efficiency of a water agitator for washing prints.

Certificates were awarded to H. F. Newell of Stonegate for enlarged photographic portraits and W. P. Glaisby of Marygate for photographs of the interior of York Minster. William Punderson Glaisby was a son of John Glaisby, proprietor of the York Repository of Arts at 9 Coney Street, a shop now occupied by the Yorkshire Evening Press. By 1872 he was working professionally from these premises; then in 1877 father and son moved to 7 Spurriergate. Glaisby continued to work as a photographer until 1902 when he became the librarian of the York Subscription Library in St. Leonards.

Such was the success of the 1866 Exhibition that another was organised in 1879, again by William Pumphrey shortly before his retirement to Bath. On this occasion the York photographers exhibiting were W. T. & R. Gowland, W. Monkhouse, W. Pumphrey and J. Duncan. Joseph Duncan was by trade a cabinet maker and worked at first, for John Taylor in Coney Street before setting up on his own at 4 Church Street. His interest in photography was aroused by the cameras, at that time made of wood, which were brought to him for repair or alteration and he began studying the practical processes of picture making in his spare time. In 1866 Duncan left cabinet making for good and took over the photographic business of Burkill & Co. (successors to S. Hoggard) at 27 Davygate. A few years afterwards he moved to Minster Gates where his Photographic Repository was well known to visitors to the City. Architecture was a special interest to him, and, after this move, being so close to the Minster, he was able to make many negatives of it illustrating different points of view and details of its various parts. On his death on 18 September 1895 at the age of 75, the firm was continued by his stepson-in-law, Edmund Lewin, under the name of Duncan and Lewin, Tourist Photographic Depot. J. W. Knowles records that Duncan's 'apparatus was far from being up to date and his methods of production were on old established lines leaving the newer fads to a younger generation'. However from the 250 negatives of his which still exist it can be seen that he stopped using collodion almost as soon as gelatine dry plates were available.

One of William Monkhouse's associates in his lithography business was Francis Bedford (1816-94), an artist, known for his *Sketches in York* 1841, *The Churches of York* c. 1843 and his illustrations in Poole & Hugall's *York Cathedral and its Antiquities* 1850. He left York to join Day & Son, a firm of lithographers in London. While working in York his employer must have introduced him to the intricacies of photography in which he became so proficient that in 1862 he was invited by the Prince of Wales to go with him on a tour of the Near East. The pictures Bedford exhibited on his return established him as a photographer and he went on to achieve a national reputation with his photographs of landscapes and architecture. He occasionally revisited York to take views of the City and to visit his old friend, William Monkhouse, who accompanied him on his photographic walks in search of subjects.

While many pictures of York in the early days of photography can be attributed to known photographers there are others which cannot but nevertheless, whether they were taken by the professionals or, indeed, by the amateurs who dabbled in the new art, they are all of value as a record of the changing face of the continuing City.

J. W. Knowles, 1860 or before: Half a pair of stereoscopic photographs of Barker Tower. To the left are the steps which were the landing place of the ferry which plied on the Ouse until Lendal Bridge, built between 1860 and 1863, was completed. On the right is the Ebor Works where Summers Varvill manufactured planes and other wood working tools until the factory was moved to North Street into a building next to St. John's church and this building demolished.

Evelyn Collection. ES 1712

J. W. Knowles, between 1847 and 1860: This half of a stereoscopic pair shows the cast iron, inverted T-girder bridge which was built in only 12 weeks in 1845 to the designs of Robert Stephenson to carry the York and North Midland Railway's Scarborough branch across the Ouse. After the collapse of a similar bridge at Chester on 24 May 1847 it was strengthened by the addition of the diagonal timber struts seated in cast shoes still in situ today. A new bridge was built on the original piers in 1875 as part of the preparatory work for the new station being constructed outside the City walls.

Mrs. Milward Knowles

Joseph Duncan, 1879, gelatine: After leaving 27 Davygate in c. 1870 Joseph Duncan for the rest of his life worked in Minster Gates in the building projecting out from the right. In the shop on the ground floor he sold to tourists photographs of York and district printed and prepared in the rooms above. On the top floor he made a glasshouse by inserting a large window, masked with paper, to provide an even source of light for his work. At the end of Stonegate Henry Hardcastle's sign records that his firm was established in 1831 contradicting the date of 1770 displayed there now. The goddess Minerva on the other side, carved in 1801 by Francis Wolstenholme as a sign for his cousin John's bookshop, advertises Bradbury's sewing machine depot, a business which later moved to Davygate.

P. W. Hanstock

Joseph Duncan, 1874: This view of
Stonegate was taken by Joseph
Duncan from a window in an upper
floor of his shop in Minster Gates.
The sign of the Star Inn proclaims
that Samuel Abbey is still the landlord.
He died in February 1874 but the sign
may not have been repainted for some
time after Harry Watson replaced
him. This is indicated by the jettied
building at its left hand end which has
already been flamboyantly decorated
by John Ward Knowles who bought it
in March 1874. To the left of the
lamp-post is the shop of one of
Duncan's rivals, photographer
Augustus Mahalski.
Evelyn Collection. ES 1754

Joseph Duncan, 1870, collodion: The original Station Hotel, completed by 1853 and Royal from 1854, is now hidden from view by Horace Field's Norman Shaw style headquarters office (1906) for the North Eastern Railway, itself now masked by the post second world war Yorkshire Insurance (now General Accident) building. The Yorkshire Club (1870) on the left of the Victorian Museum Street, created to connect Lendal Bridge (1863) with Duncombe Place (1864), has only just opened, while the site of George Fowler Jones' slightly later Club Chambers on the corner of Lendal is marked by hoardings covered with fly posters. *P. W. Hanstock*

Joseph Duncan, c. 1870, collodion: The market cross in Pavement, built by Thomas Mann for the executors of Marmaduke Rawden in 1671 and taken down in 1813, has been exchanged for a roofless urinal, resplendent with its own gas lamp, one of many provided in the City at that time for the convenience of gentlemen (there were no similar facilities for ladies). Its underground replacement at the end of Parliament Street was built in 1894 and extended in 1927. G. E. Street's design for the east end of All Saints church, realised in 1887, changed the two light windows at the ends of the side aisle to three lights. *P. W. Hanstock*

Joseph Duncan, c. 1870, collodion: Railings were put round Clifton Green about 1905 – prior to that the green had been open on all sides but before the pond in the Burdyke was drained and filled in it had been protected by similar railings. George Fowler Jones' church, dedicated to St. Philip and St. James, still stands in isolation. The splendidly grotesque, grey-white brick St. James' Terrace that now stands on its right hand side was built c. 1879. It was originally St. Philip's Terrace but gained its present name in 1890 to avoid confusion with St. James' Terrace, Fulford Road.

P. W. Hanstock

Joseph Duncan, 1876, collodion: This picture can be dated much more closely, in fact to Wednesday, 3 May 1876 when the *York Herald*, advertised on one of the boards leaning against St. Sampson's churchyard wall, was published. This with the other boards advertising the *Yorkshire Post*, the *Leeds Mercury* and a sale of work in the Lendal chapel have been placed there by Robert Gilbertson whose newsagent's shop is just off the picture to the right on the other side of Silver Street. The late medieval St. Sampson's church was, except for the tower, rebuilt in 1846-8. The upper stage of the tower was, however, removed then and not replaced until 1907-9. The church closed for regular worship in 1968 and re-opened as an Old People's Centre in 1974.

P. W. Hanstock

Joseph Duncan, 1873, collodion: Most photographers when making a picture of Bootham Bar stand near the Art Gallery and include the Minster in their composition. By moving in close not only has Duncan concentrated attention on the bar but he has heightened the feeling of awe and invincibility which must have been experienced by its attackers. In later years and before the external staircase giving access to the footway along the walls was built in 1889 the wall to the right became an advertising hoarding but here there is only one poster proclaiming the attractions of the Grand Yorkshire Gala to be held on 18, 19 and 20 June 1873.

P. W. Hanstock

Joseph Duncan, c. 1876, collodion: Museum Street presents a somewhat austere face to the Museum Gardens of the Yorkshire Philosophical Society on the other side. Next to Thomas's Hotel (extreme left) is the triple arched entrance to the Festival Concert Rooms symmetrically placed between two three-bayed wings. From the early 17th century this street was called Lendal Street. Because of the confusion with nearby Lendal a proposal was made to the City Commissioners in 1842 that its name be changed to Museum Street. The Commissioners responded by calling both streets Lendal but, as the change had been made by 1851, obviously had had second thoughts. *P. W. Hanstock*

Joseph Duncan, 1876, collodion: The photographer has taken his camera to a vantage point that had only just become available – the roof of the new Royal Station Hotel (opened for business 20 May 1878). The Minster rises out of a foreground composed largely of new buildings that are a consequence of the road improvements made necessary by the opening of Lendal bridge in 1863. On the left, to an extent overshadowed by the Minster itself, is the Roman Catholic church of St. Wilfrid, consecrated 2 June 1864, and on the right, behind Lendal tower, Club Chambers and the slightly earlier Yorkshire Club of 1870. The rubble of Summers Varvill's Ebor Works can be seen on the near bank of the river.

P. W. Hanstock

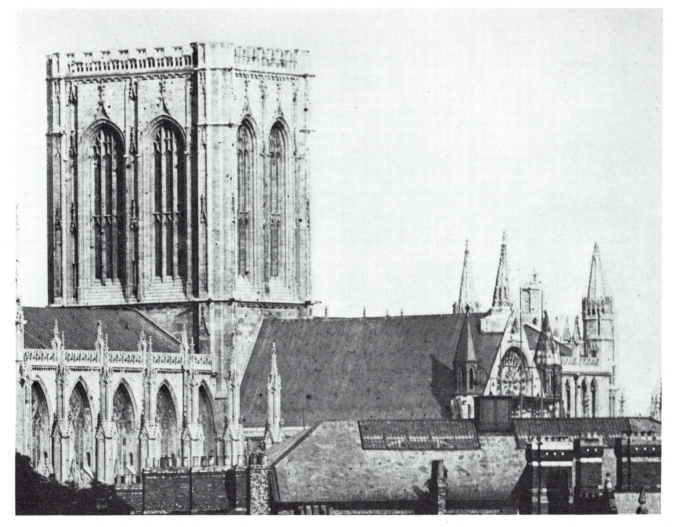

Joseph Duncan, 1876, collodion: Such is the sharpness of Duncan's negatives that enlargements can be made without loosing any quality, bringing to light interesting details. On 16 October 1876 G. E. Street, consulting architect to the Dean and Chapter, wrote to Dean Duncombe 'The Pinnacles [at the end of the south transept of the Minster] are now in course of execution, their proportions having been first of all decided by the erection of a rough full size model and we have found the whole of the evidence necessary for the restoration of the three gables over the south doorway.' This enlargement shows these models of the pinnacles very clearly over the roof of the Festival Concert Rooms. *P. W. Hanstock*

Joseph Duncan, 1870, collodion: The Yorkshire Club was established in 1838 originating from the Yorkshire Union Hunt Club. Having outgrown its first home in St. Leonard's Place it held two competitions for the design of new premises to be built in Museum Street alongside the approach road to Lendal bridge. C. J. Parnell of London was the eventual winner in 1868 and a red brick building with white stone dressings was erected to his design. At the left the Lendal chapel of Charles Watson and James Pigott Pritchett has not yet been obscured by George Fowler Jones' Club Chambers.

P. W. Hanstock

Joseph Duncan, c. 1876, collodion: As Coney Street is deserted and the shop windows are all shuttered this photograph must have been taken on a summer Sunday morning – the clock on St. Martin le Grand church, resplendent with its new bracket (1856) and a black face, stands at twenty three minutes past six o'clock. Behind the clock is the original shop of Leak and Thorpe (1869) who have not yet spread into the adjacent premises of George Balmforth, dyer and cleaner. On the other side of the street is the tall building, pulled down in 1961, of Italian warehouseman, Samuel Border.   *P. W. Hanstock*

Joseph Duncan, c. 1876, collodion: Although devoid of all pedestrians and vehicles except for a solitary wheelbarrow the shops in Goodramgate are open for business. The butcher on the right is still displaying his meat in the medieval fashion of The Shambles, in an open shop front with a bench under a small fixed canopy to keep off the worst of the weather. Lady Row still, as now, has its timber framework hidden by plaster, although for a time in the early years of this century the woodwork was exposed. *P. W. Hanstock*

Joseph Duncan, c. 1880, gelatine: Between 1705 and 1946 St. Anthony's Hall in Peaseholme Green housed the York Blue Coat Boys' School founded to lodge, feed and educate boys, particularly orphans, between the ages of seven and twelve. They were to be trained in some practical skill and then apprenticed for service on ships of war. The great hall was used as the school room where several classes were taught simultaneously in separate areas. One master, teaching the class in front of the organ, had the benefit of a stove next to his desk.

P. W. Hanstock

John Lardon Draffin, c. 1864: The cleared area on the City side of Duncombe Place has been newly laid out with a lawn and fenced with simple iron railings. The house at the extreme right, replaced soon afterwards by the building which is now the Dean Court Hotel, was occupied at the time this picture was taken by a Homeopathic Dispensary which by 1867 had moved to Stonegate and eventually found its home in Burgin's chemist shop in Coney Street.

Evelyn Collection. ES 2727

William Monkhouse, 1866: In 1851 William Pumphrey visited the Great Exhibition which inspired him to suggest a similar event in York. Thus the Yorkshire Fine Art and Industrial Exhibition was held from 24 July to 2 November 1866 in an ornate but temporary building, designed by Edward Taylor in consultation with J. B. and W. Atkinson, in the grounds of Bootham Park Hospital. It was constructed entirely of timber and glass and the front was decorated with the Royal arms and those of the noble patrons.

William Monkhouse, 1866: In the centre was a Grand Hall 195ft. long and 80ft. broad with a gallery 18ft. wide all round. It was lighted from the roof as the windows at each end were filled with stained glass. Behind was an annex of 9,000 square ft. for the exhibition of machinery and carriages. In all 380,691 people visited the exhibition, ensuring its financial success. The profit of £2,240 was used to establish a permanent exhibition building, the present Art Gallery, also designed by Edward Taylor, which was first used for a second Fine Art and Industrial Exhibition in 1879.

William Monkhouse, 1866: Two picture galleries 60ft. long and 30ft. wide each terminated by a pavilion 40ft. square were on either side of the Grand Hall. These housed the Fine Art exhibits, including photography. The pictures have been arranged so that every square inch of available wall space is used!

Henry F. Newell, 1866: On Thursday, 9 August 1866 the Prince and Princess of Wales with their two children came to York to visit the Yorkshire Fine Arts and Industrial Exhibition and the Yorkshire Agricultural Society's annual show and hold a grand review of the Volunteer Force on the Knavesmire. The Bars and buildings in the City were decorated for the visit and triumphal arches were erected in the streets, including Bootham, through which the royal procession passed.

Evelyn Collection. ES 1202

Henry F. Newell, 1866: This carte de visite picture of the arch at the Museum Street end of St. Leonard's Place was sold as a souvenir of the royal visit. Despite its lack of sharpness it is a valuable record of the expense the City was prepared to go to in welcoming the Prince and Princess of Wales. In the foreground the large area of cobbles shows how the majority of the streets in the City were surfaced in the middle of the last century. The racket raised by the passage of iron tyred, horse drawn vehicles over them must have been extraordinary.

Augustus Mahalski, 1866: Another carte de visite shows the decorations on the gates of the Dean's Park where the City Prize Band waits to play its part in greeting the royal visitors. Behind the railings the Deanery (1827–1939) can be seen.

Evelyn Collection. ES 1214

Anonymous, 1866: There were other arches on Lendal and Ouse bridges. The royal party stayed with Archbishop Thomson at Bishopthorpe Palace which was reached from the railway station by a route through the city centre crossing both bridges. This triumphal arch on Ouse bridge although looking very permanent was made of wood. It was designed by George Fowler Jones, built by Weatherley and Rymer and painted by T. Worthington.

Evelyn Collection. ES 1795

Anonymous, before 1879: Bootham Bar lost its barbican in July 1831 when St. Leonard's Place was constructed connecting Bootham to Museum Street. The building between the Bar and Queen Margaret's arch (on the right), together with the Bird in Hand public house, which it obscures, were pulled down to create Exhibition Square in front of the Art Gallery, opened in 1879. The Bird in Hand transferred to a building on the opposite side of Bootham and changed its name to The Exhibition. The narrow entrance to Gillygate (on the left) was widened in 1910 by the demolition of the two shops on the side nearest the Bar. This allowed a better alignment for the tramlines to Haxby.

Evelyn Collection. ES 2315

Anonymous, 1862: The narrow entrance into the newly constructed Foss Islands Road is concealed by the buildings on the right but, strangely, there is a clear, unobstructed view into Walmgate. In 1862 part of the wall and a small arch of 1804, adjacent to the bar, were removed and replaced by the present much larger arch. This photograph was taken during the progress of the work. Foss Islands Road was built across the swamp that was once the fishpond of the Foss. Following the purchase of the Foss Navigation in 1854 the Corporation drained the swamp and made the new road across it.

Evelyn Collection. ES 1195

Anonymous, 1863: A single arch of 1753 on the left hand side of Micklegate Bar was replaced by two arches in 1863, the same year that St. Thomas' Hospital (extreme right) moved to a new building (now The Moat Hotel) adjacent to Victoria Bar in Nunnery Lane. To the left of the hospital is the Punch Bowl under the tenancy of George Howard from June 1863. A stage coach, a reminder of a means of long distance transport that was killed off by the coming of the railways in 1840, stands outside the Windmill Hotel (extreme left) beyond which is a building which was demolished in 1907 to widen Queen Street ready for the advent of the electric trams.   *Evelyn Collection. ES 1801*

J. Beckett, Scarborough, before 1860 (Stereograph 23): Whilst the foreground is cluttered with the buildings, coaldrops and sidings of the York and North Midland Railway leading right down to the river, the view of the Minster is not yet marred by St. Wilfrid's Roman Catholic Church, although it is partially obstructed by the Festival Concert Rooms built in 1825 behind the Assembly Rooms. The City walls were not breached until January 1874 when the first of the two arches giving better access to the new railway station outside the walls was constructed. The second, opposite the Railway Offices, followed in 1876.

Sydney Heppell

Anonymous, 1863: Many years passed after the opening of Lendal Bridge on 8 January 1863 before The Esplanade was planted with trees and the river bank formalised. In front of the Museum Gardens railings, erected by John Walker in 1844, stands a lady in a crinoline, a style of dress which had vanished by 1870. The parentage of Lendal Bridge in Thomas Page's earlier Westminster Bridge (1862) can be seen in the spandrels, balustrade and lamp standards.

Evelyn Collection. ES 2321

Anonymous, between 1849 and 1860: The steps of the ferry landing in Museum Street are to the right of Lendal Tower and behind them the house which was demolished to make way for the Yorkshire Club (built 1870). The Tower was given its crenellations in 1849 or shortly afterwards when George Townsend Andrew restored it to its original height after removing the tank which for so many years was the basis of the City's water supply.

Evelyn Collection. ES 870

Anonymous, before 1871: The south door of the Minster before G. E. Street undertook his restoration of the transept. The clock, installed in 1750 by Henry Hindley, a York clockmaker, was removed in 1871. Twelve years later, in 1883, it was re-erected in its present position in the north transept, with, from its medieval predecessor two oak men at arms to strike the four quarters. The crossed keys over the clock face allude to St. Peter, the patron saint of the Minster. This picture may possibly have been taken by Francis Bedford and published by F. Frith & Co.   *P. W. Hanstock*

Anonymous, c. 1870: This large house, North Lodge, standing in its own grounds was in 1870 the home of John Close, an iron founder and winemerchant. As it stood just outside the walls where the N.E.R. wished to build their new station (completed 1877) he was persuaded to leave by the offer of the railway company to build him a new house, The Hollies (now the Chase Hotel) on the then city boundary at Dringhouses. *Evelyn Collection. ES 335*

Appendix

18. Thomas Spencer died 21 Jan. 1881 aged 70		51 Fossgate	D.1861 – Jan. 1881	Business taken over by Mark Midgley.
19. Richard Wright died 17 Dec. 1884 aged 70	Artist	14 Spurriergate	D.1861 – D.1865	
20. Burkill & Co.		27 Davygate	Sept. 1862 – 1866	Succeeded S. Hoggard (q.v.). Photographic business taken over by Joseph Duncan (q.v.).
21. Robert Place	Photographer & Tobacconist	3 Railway Street	Nov. 1862 – D.1887	Succeeded G. Brown (q.v.).
22. William Monkhouse	Lithographer	4 Lendal	D.1865 – D.1879	Learnt photography with William Pumphrey. Photographic business taken over by William Eskett (q.v.).
23. Henry Bramham		14 Colliergate	D.1867 – D.1889	
24. John T. Brown		7 Little Stonegate	D.1867	
25. Matthew Cuthbert born 1838		19 & 20 Davygate	D.1867 – D.1895	Matthew Cuthbert & Son D.1893. Cecil Cuthbert D. 1895.
26. Joseph Duncan died 18 Sept. 1895 aged 75	Cabinet Maker	27 Davygate Minster Gates	1866 – D.1867 D.1872 – D.1921	Succeeded Burkill & Co. (q.v.). Photographic Repository from D.1876. Duncan & Lewin D.1896/7 – Edmund F. Lewin was his stepson-in-law.
27. William Hardman born Apr. 1836		82 Micklegate	D.1867 – D.1881/2	Photographic chemist, 17 New Bridge Street November 1862.
28. William Sayer died 27 Jan. 1904	Newsagent	101 Goodramgate 15 Fishergate	D.1867 – D.1887 D.1893 – D.1895	
29. Henry Browne born 10 Dec. 1837, died 1 Jan. 1917		21 Blake Street 57 then 28 Stonegate	D.1872 – D.1881/2 D.1885 – D.1887	Son of John Browne, the Minster Historian.
30. William Punderson Glaisby		9 Coney Street 7 Spurriergate 9 South Parade Museum Street	D.1872 – D.1876 D.1879 – D.1895 D.1896/7 – D.1900/1 D.1902	Son of John Glaisby, proprietor of a Repository of Arts in Coney Street from July 1848 – May 1877 and Spurriergate May 1877 – Dec. 1887.
31. Thomas Brooks		10 then 14 Spurriergate 24 Coney Street 12 Micklegate	D.1872 D.1879 – D.1881/2 D.1885 – D.1889	Brook Bros. D. 1883.
32. William Bullivant		2 Orchard Street	D.1872	
33. William Eskett		1 Garden Street, Groves 5 Lendal	D.1872 D.1879 – D.1900/1	Succeeded William Monkhouse (q.v.).
34. Watson Chapman died 7 Nov. 1877	Bookseller & Photographic Repository	Minster Gates	D.1876	Mrs. Annie Chapman D.1883. Miss W. Chapman D.1895. Miss Georgiana Chapman D.1909.

D – Directory

GEORGE BROWN'S
PHOTOGRAPHIC DEPÔT,
No. 3, RAILWAY-STREET, YORK.

First Class PORTRAITS taken Daily, either for the Stereoscope, or in the ordinary way.

COLOURED AND PLAIN CALOTYPES ON PAPER.

COLLODION PICTURES ON GLASS,

EITHER PLAIN OR IN COLOURS, BY GEORGE BROWN'S NEW PROCESS.

Every Requisite for Artists or Amateurs, at wholesale prices.

TRADE CATALOGUES GRATIS.

A Choice Selection of **VIEWS of YORK** and **YORKSHIRE**, for the Stereoscope, 1s. 6d. each.

☞ *Instructions in every department of Photography.*

John Sampson, *Handbook for York,* c. 1860.

NOTICE!
A. MAHALSKI,
PHOTOGRAPHIC ARTIST.
34, Goodramgate, YORK,

Has much pleasure in announcing to the Public, that he has built a NEW COMFORTABLE PORTRAIT GALLERY, which affords him the advantage of taking Portraits in all Seasons and Weathers.

Portraits taken from the Largest size to the Smallest, for Brooches, Pins, Lockets, or Rings; and also Portraits on Cloth, Paper, or Tin, suitable to send by Post, on very reasonable Terms.

☞ **A respectable Portrait for 1s.**

N.B.—Portraits Copied the same size as the Original.

Advertisement c. 1860.

PHOTOGRAPHS
AT
MINSTER GATES & THE LODGE,
LENDAL BRIDGE.

Large Assortment of City & County Views.

NEW PHOTOGRAPHS
OF
Castle Howard, Wressle, Nun Monckton, Hemingbro', York Minster, &c.

A WELL SELECTED STOCK OF

White Wood Goods with Microscopic Views.
MAY BE HAD AT
J. DUNCAN'S.

George Stevens, *Directory for 1881–1882 of the City of York etc.*

HENRY BROWNE,
Catholic Bookseller, Stationer, & Photographer,
21, BLAKE STREET, YORK.

Agent for the "Catholic Times," "Universe," "Weekly Register," "Irishman," "Young Ireland," "Dublin Weekly News," &c., &c.

Prayer Books, Hymn Books, Rosary Beads, Crosses, Scapulars, Statuettes, Lace Pictures, Note Paper, Envelopes, Memorandums, Books, Pencils, Steel Pens, &c., &c., always in stock.

Brownes "History of the Metropolitan Church of St. Peter's of York." Also abstracts from the Fabric Rolls of York Minster, by John Browne.

The Photographic Studio is open daily from 10 a.m. to 5 p.m. VIEWS TAKEN IN TOWN OR COUNTRY.

THE ONLY CATHOLIC BOOKSELLER IN YORK.
H. BROWNE, 21, Blake Street.

George Stevens, *Directory for 1881–1882 of the City of York etc.*

Index of Photographs